SHOES

SHOES

AN ILLUSTRATED HISTORY

REBECCA SHAWCROSS

BLOOMSBURY

LONDON · NEW DELHI · NEW YORK · SYDNEY

Bloomsbury Visual Arts

An imprint of Bloomsbury Publishing Plc

50 Bedford Square	1385 Broadway
London	New York
WC1B 3DP	NY 10018
UK	USA

www.bloomsbury.com

**Bloomsbury is a registered trade mark of
Bloomsbury Publishing Plc**

British Library Cataloguing-in-Publication Data
A catalogue record for this book is available from the British Library.

ISBN: 978-1-47253-100-1

Editorial director: Will Steeds
Senior editor: Laura Ward
Project editor: Anna Southgate
Book design: Paul Palmer-Edwards, Grade Design, London
Commissioned photography: John Chase
Picture research: Susannah Jayes
Indexer: Cheryl Hunston
Colour reproduction: Pixel Colour Imaging, London

Manufactured in China

CONTENTS

INTRODUCTION

Who could fail to admire the skill and craftsmanship involved in making a bespoke pair of brogues? Or swoon with desire at a diamond-encrusted vertiginous heel? Who hasn't dreamt of owning the latest pair of Manolo Blahniks? All of us, perhaps, but what drives this seemingly universal obsession with shoes – an obsession that sees us coveting footwear past and present in ways that no other form of clothing is lusted after?

It should not be surprising to discover that there is no straightforward answer to this question, but rather a series of answers that become apparent as we examine humankind's long and intricate relationship with shoes. For this obsession is not a modern phenomenon, but goes back much further and runs much deeper than a passing fancy for the latest designer labels and catwalk styles.

A UNIQUE DUALITY

This footwear fascination ties, to some extent, to its duality. At one extreme, shoes are nothing more than practical outer coverings for the feet – at their most basic level they serve to keep our feet warm and dry in cold and wet conditions, and provide comfort and protection from the hazards of rough terrain. Yet at the other extreme, a pair of shoes might be embellished with all manner of showy decoration – its design highly impractical, fragile even, and serving little more purpose than to satisfy the vanity or sheer bravado of the wearer.

Time and again during the course of footwear history, this dual aspect of shoes – the practical versus the indulgent – has come to the fore. Over the centuries, we have seen footwear designed for very specific purposes. Consider, for example, the Roman caliga, a leather marching shoe that was hobnailed for better grip, or the eighteenth-century thick, leather postilion boot destined for long-distance riding or Adi Dassler's spiked running shoes championed by the sports heroes of the 1930s. When called upon to produce footwear of lasting durability or technical ingenuity, designers have rarely failed to come up with the goods. Such examples often arise out of necessity and we frequently see indulgent designs wane in times of hardship or austerity – immediately following the French Revolution of the 1790s or during the First and Second World Wars, for example – resulting in pared back, practical designs.

Similar observations can be made in the case of indulgence, the most obvious of which has to be the addition of the platform, and then the heel. From as early as the chopine of the Middle Ages, we have found height alluring, both as wearers and onlookers. Who doesn't feel a frisson of excitement at gaining a few centimetres, often despite the inevitable discomfort?

Heel evolution was relatively slow to start, in part owing to the technical challenges it posed to the shoemaker, and it wasn't until the 1950s that we saw the stiletto – now a staple of the modern wardrobe. The heel is not the only indulgence to have emerged over the centuries, and shoes have long been made from exquisite textiles, or with buckles, bows and roses – often designed with a flair and flamboyance that far exceeds their practical use.

AN INDICATION OF STATUS

It was not that long ago – in terms of shoe history, at least – that a new pair of shoes was available only to the wealthiest or highest-ranking members of society. All shoes were handmade by skilled craftsmen, often using prohibitively expensive materials, and this took time and money. As such it was inevitable that shoes were seen as status symbols, certainly throughout the medieval and Renaissance periods but also through the seventeenth and eighteenth centuries and well into the nineteenth. One's choice of footwear was an instant indication of social status and wealth. It even went some way towards establishing one's identity, character and – in the case of the medieval poulaine (and, later, the winklepicker of the 1950s) – one's sexual proclivities, too.

The mass production of the industrial age that started in the mid-nineteenth century brought an end to the exclusivity of owning a new pair of shoes (although today, a pair of bespoke shoes remains financially out of reach for most). Shoes nevertheless continue to reveal a great deal about one's identity. For many, the decision to purchase a new pair of shoes is not only a monetary one, but one that consciously or subconsciously considers one's identity. Not only do the shoes we choose to wear represent our perception of ourselves, but also – harking back to the status symbols of the past – how we would like others to perceive us and our role within society. Returning to stiletto heels – particularly those of the power-dressed 1980s – there are few things that rival their potency, all glamour,

BELOW: These silk damask mules date from around 1720 and are thought to be French. The French have always been considered primary arbiters of taste and style when it comes to fashion. From the fifteenth to the eighteenth centuries the latest styles from France were frequently adopted and copied across Europe.

strength, domination and sexuality rolled into one. Is it any wonder, therefore, that we are so obsessed with shoes? Not only do we agonize over what to buy for ourselves, but we are constantly looking to see what anyone else is wearing in order to assess the kinds of people they are (or the kinds of people they want us to think they are).

It is also interesting to note that even those people who say they are not interested in shoes, and simply pick practical examples because they have to wear something, are sending out particular messages of their own.

DEGREES OF INTIMACY

If you've ever worn a pair of someone else's shoes, you will remember how odd and uncomfortable they felt. Even if the shoes were identical to yours, they would have felt alien because, more than any other item of clothing, shoes become permanently moulded to the unique shape of their owner's feet. It is precisely because of this that we tend to develop intimate relationships with our shoes, remembering old favourites with tenderness and grieving over their loss when they can no longer be worn.

A well worn shoe captures the very essence of its wearer and, although he or she may be long gone, his or her personal imprint has been captured for all time. Consider how readily a child will dress up in his or her parents' shoes, for example, pretending to be Mum or Dad for five minutes. And then think about how rare it is to find someone who would willingly step into the shoes of the dead. This is perhaps an act of such intimacy that it is seen, quite literally, as taking a step too far.

There is great intimacy, too, in the act of concealing shoes, often within the fabric of a building – a tradition seen in many world cultures, going back thousands of years. In almost all cases the concealed shoes are those of children. They also tend to be incredibly well worn, the wearer's spirit remaining within the shoe – contained by its shape. Perhaps their spirit is tasked with repelling evil spectres that may try to harm a house and its occupants.

SYMBOLISM IN SHOES

Proof that our obsession with shoes is both long-standing and global can be found in the symbolic roles that shoes have played – and continue to play – in many world cultures. From the keeping of a child's first ever shoes as a memento of just how tiny his or her feet once were to the various roles shoes play in wedding ceremonies, footwear features frequently to mark significant, life-changing events. For example, shoes play a major role in coming-of-age ceremonies across the world. Latin American traditions include the quinceañera, a celebration of a girl's fifteenth birthday. This birthday is observed differently from those of previous years, as it marks the transition from childhood to womanhood. During the quinceañera ceremony, 'the changing of the shoe' involves the girl's father removing her flat shoe in exchange for a high-heeled one, so representing the transition into adulthood.

At Greek weddings today, names are written in the soles of the bride's shoes. Those that remain by the end of the day indicate the number of children the bride will have, or, in some traditions, suggest which of her friends will marry next.

In ancient China, 'longevity shoes' embroidered with a lotus flower and a ladder were worn by the dead to guide them to the afterlife, while banging shoes against a doorway is a way of calling wandering souls to return.

SINCE ANCIENT TIMES

We know that humans have been wearing shoes for many thousands of years, as evidenced by the discovery of sandals in Missouri, United States, that date back to almost eight thousand years ago. Since that time footwear has evolved in ways barely imaginable to the shoemakers of ancient times.

In celebration of our deep-rooted obsession with shoes, and exploring many of the themes discussed above, *Shoes: An Illustrated History* offers a lavishly illustrated chronology of the shoe's development from ancient times to the present.

Focusing primarily on the prevailing styles of the last one thousand years, this book charts the colourful progression from straw-filled moccasins through to embroidered mules and elegant court shoes, and dashing co-respondents to Christian Louboutin's glossy red soles.

Written by museum curator Rebecca Shawcross, the book highlights leading developments in style and technology, and discusses the major political, social and economic events that have influenced shoe design over the centuries. Charming in their own right, the many stories told combine with wonderful footwear anecdotes to reveal how different shoe styles were perceived in their day.

BELOW: This amazing Dragon shoe was designed and made by Thea Cadabra in 1979. Cadabra's designs strike a perfect balance between art and traditional shoemaking. Handcrafted in the finest leather, these exquisite shoes are elaborate, yet eminently wearable.

I

THE FIRST SHOES

THE ORIGINS OF FOOTWEAR

The precise origins of footwear are unknown. There are no recorded dates as to when people began to wear shoes of any kind, nor do we know the names of the very first people to wear them. However, through recent discoveries of preserved footwear, and from pictorial representations such as ancient Etruscan frescoes, we know that footwear has existed since prehistoric times.

Early footwear was largely dependent on location. In hot countries there was a need to protect feet from rough terrain, but also to keep them cool. A form of sandal was the obvious answer. In cold climates the need to keep feet warm was paramount, and so more robust forms of footwear developed. In all regions, we know that early man used the skins of slaughtered animals for clothing – and also for making shoes.

Whatever the origins of the earliest shoes, the development of footwear over the centuries has led to surprisingly few different shoe styles. Although the debate rages as to how many true shoe types there are, it inevitably boils down to just seven or eight: the sandal, the moccasin, the court shoe, the lace shoe, the monk, the leg boot, the bar shoe, the clog and the mule.

OPPOSITE: The sandals found at the Arnold Research Cave, Missouri were made using dried leaves that were moulded into cord and woven, rather like an espadrille. The average length of the footwear was 26.5 cm (10½ in), so similar to an adult size today.

PREHISTORIC SANDALS

Sandals are recognized as the first form of footwear ever worn and their history goes back to ancient times. The earliest known examples were relatively simple creations, made from the natural materials to hand – leaves, twisted vines and woven palms. Given the nature of these materials, most early sandals are likely to have worn out quickly with use, but they were at least relatively easy to replace. Over the years, and through experimentation, shoes became robust enough to wear for a reasonable length of time. Even so, the fibrous materials used for making such sandals were perishable and decomposed quickly, which is why very few early examples survive today.

In light of this, the survival of several prehistoric sandals – discovered in the 1950s in the Arnold Research Cave, located in central Missouri in the United States – is astounding. The sandals were among a group of shoes found at the site, collectively dating from eight hundred to eight thousand years old. By far the oldest among them, the sandals are made from fibrous materials including the local yucca-like plant known as rattlesnake master, which could be woven in to a tough fabric that was used to construct the top and bottom of the footwear. The temperature, humidity and dry conditions within the cave contributed to the survival of these shoes.

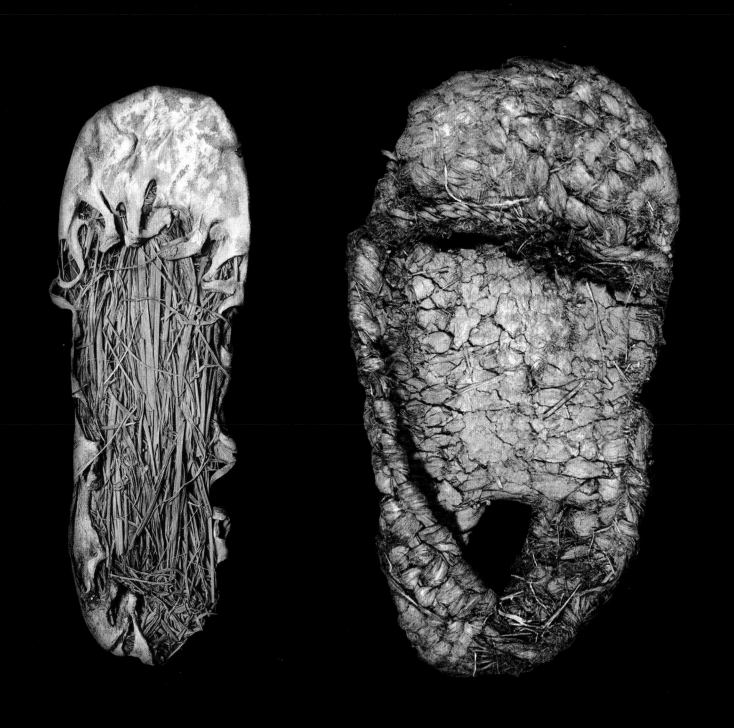

THE OLDEST SHOE DISCOVERY

In 2010 a shoe discovered in a cave in Armenia proved to date back as far 3500 BCE – the oldest shoe ever found. Appearing in a *National Geographic* magazine article, it was described thus: 'Stuffed with grass, perhaps as an insulator or an early shoe tree, the 5,500-year-old moccasin-like shoe was found exceptionally well preserved – thanks to a surfeit of sheep dung'.

The shoe appears to have been made from a single piece of cowhide and bears a striking resemblance to the Aran Isle pampootie (see below). It is laced along the seams at the front and back, with a leather cord to pull it tight. Whether the straw was for insulation, an early form of crude sock or just randomly placed remains a mystery.

HOW THE SHOE WAS MADE

The construction of the shoe is incredibly basic: the wearer placed his or her foot on a flat piece of damp leather, which was then folded around the foot and sewn. While Tudor shoes are often referred to as 'footbags', owing to their broad-toed appearance (see p. 33), this shoe is quite literally a foot bag. The Armenian shoe is a rough Size 5 (US 7, European 38). By today's standards, this would make it a woman's shoe, but it could equally have been that of a small man or a younger person.

  Similar constructions include the deerskin moccasins traditionally worn by Native Americans and, from the late nineteenth century, rabbit-skin moccasins used by the Aborigines of South Australia.

OPPOSITE: A pair of Shetland-made, cured cowhide rivlins. These reproductions, made in 1968, are a close imitation of much earlier examples dating back to the early Bronze Age in Northern Europe.

THE PAMPOOTIE

The pampootie, also known as a rivlin, is one of the earliest known styles of leather shoe. A primitive footbag or a crude example of a European moccasin, it was fashioned from hairy rawhide. Each shoe was made from a single piece of rawhide, which was folded around the foot when still fresh and stitched together using a length of twine. The rawhide usually came from the animal's buttocks, where the hide tends to be thicker. It was also usual to cut the hide so that the hair lay with its roots facing the heel – to provide a better grip when walking. The pampootie is a style of shoe that survived in the Aran Islands, off the west coast of Ireland, right up to the early twentieth century.

ÖTZI'S SHOE

Until the discovery of the Armenian cave shoe in 2010 (see p. 14), a leather shoe discovered in Europe's Ötztal Alps ranked as the world's oldest. It was found on the body of a well-preserved man, Ötzi, thought to have lived around 3300 BCE and named after his location on the border between Austria and Italy. His body, his clothing and his belongings – including the shoe – are on display in the South Tyrol Museum of Archaeology, Italy.

The shoe is a sophisticated design that consists of two parts. Within an outer shoe made from deerskin sits an inner shoe composed of grass netting – its purpose was to hold hay in place for insulation. Both parts of the shoe are fastened with leather straps to an oval-shaped sole made from bearskin. The deerskin upper is constructed with the fur on the outside. The shaft around the ankle is bound with grass fibres and a strip of leather is attached diagonally across the sole to give better grip. In recent discussions on the shoe's purpose, British archaeologist Jacqui Woods has hypothesized that they are actually the upper part of snowshoes. Further items were found during Ötzi's discovery, including what was thought at the time to be a backpack. Subsequent research by Jacqui Woods, which she presented in her 2005 paper entitled 'Backpack or Showshoes? A New Perspective on an Otzi Artefact', points to the idea that this 'backpack' was in fact the wooden frame and netting of a snowshoe.

In recent times, Professor Petr Hlavacek, Czech academic and footwear technologist at Tomas Bata University, reproduced a limited edition of the shoe totalling five pairs. Once Hlavacek had made the shoes, he and a fellow mountaineer tested them over a two-day hike in the Austrian Alps. They found them remarkably practical and satisfactory even in such cold conditions. Although the shoes themselves were not waterproof, the grass insulation kept their feet warm even when wet. On studying the footwear, he commented that, '…because the shoes are actually quite complex, I'm convinced that even 5,300 years ago, people had the equivalent of a cobbler [shoemaker] who made shoes for other people.'

WHO WAS ÖTZI?

The remarkable preservation of Ötzi, his clothes, footwear, ornaments and tools provides us with a fascinating glimpse of what life might have been like for a person living during the Copper Age.

Ötzi appears to have carried extensive personal belongings with him, allowing him to remain away from home for long periods of time. He would also have been self-reliant, using tools to hunt animals, repair damaged items and make new ones when necessary.

His personal belongings included a copper-bladed axe, dagger, bow, quiver and backpack. He was wearing a goat-hide coat, loincloth and goatskin leggings. The leggings, possibly the oldest ever discovered, covered the thigh and calf. Laces sewn at the top enabled the leggings to be tied to a belt in order to prevent them falling down. Ötzi sported a bearskin hat and a calf-hide belt and pouch. The pouch contained a scraper, drill and flint flake used for a variety of possible jobs, including sewing.

Ötzi's copper axe provides an important clue about his social standing. Such items were status symbols during the Copper Age, indicating that the carrier was from the warrior or leadership class. Though it is hard to proffer a definitive answer, there are several theories as to what role Ötzi might have played in his community. These include a shaman who had ascended in to the mountains to carry out his priestly duties, a mineral prospector looking for ore deposits in the mountains, a hunter or a shepherd or migratory herder. It is also thought that he was fleeing up into the mountains to escape from possible attacks as his wounds indicate that he may have been involved in a fight prior to his death.

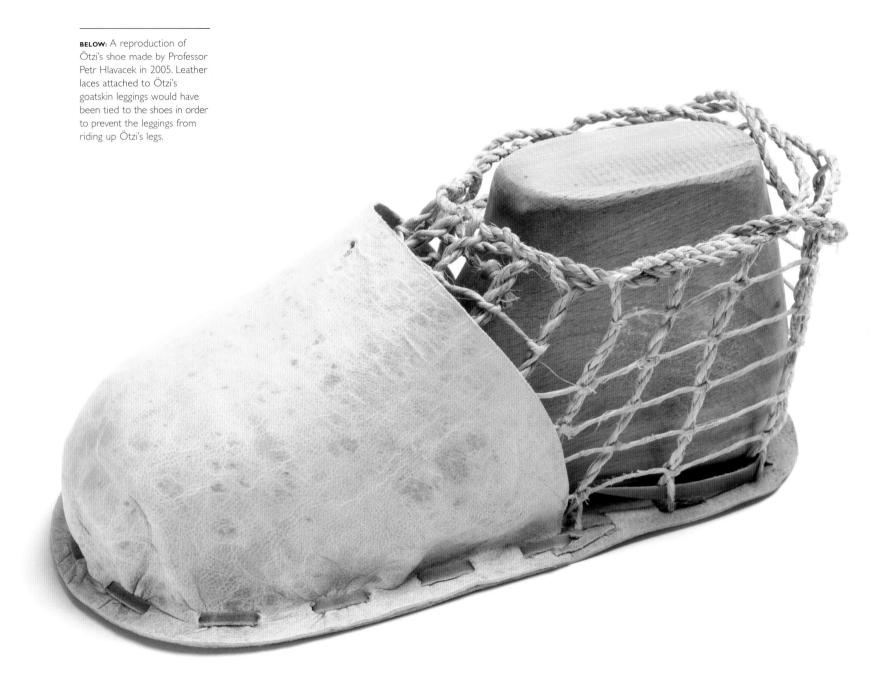

BELOW: A reproduction of Ötzi's shoe made by Professor Petr Hlavacek in 2005. Leather laces attached to Ötzi's goatskin leggings would have been tied to the shoes in order to prevent the leggings from riding up Ötzi's legs.

THE ANCIENTS

Examples of footwear survive from both ancient Egypt and ancient Rome. In fact, sufficient numbers survive to show that, particularly in the case of the ancient Romans, a variety of different styles existed and were often worn according to one's position in society.

ANCIENT EGYPT

In Egypt, it appears that all levels of society wore sandals, usually woven from papyrus, which was easily sourced. Although not as common, sandals were also made from leather, stitched with papyrus twine. One of the earliest representations of ancient Egyptian sandals is on the Narmer Palette, currently held at the Egyptian Museum in Cairo. Dating from around the thirty-first century BCE, the palette depicts the ancient Egyptian pharaoh Narmer, followed by a servant carrying his sandals.

ANCIENT ROME

Whether a non-citizen, citizen, senator, priest or soldier, all Romans were duty bound to wear the correct footwear. Typical was the Roman sandal (known at the time as a shoe) worn by Roman soldiers. When the Romans arrived in Britain during the first century CE, soldiers were wearing the military caliga – a style with open toes and an upper with a lattice pattern made from one piece of leather seamed at the back. This was a practical style, strong and well ventilated for endless marching; it was also hobnailed for longer wear and better grip. To this day, the Roman 'gladiator' sandal continues to influence shoe design and frequently appears on the catwalk.

The ancient Romans also wore a closed shoe – the calceus – which enclosed the foot, completely covering the toes and fastening with straps around the ankle. Their colour gave an indication of social standing: black for a high official, purple for nobility. The emperor and high-ranking officials wore the campagus, an open-toed boot, laced at the front.

ABOVE: An Etruscan fresco from the Tomb of Leopard at Tarquinia, c. fifth century CE, in which the musicians are wearing sandals.

ABOVE: A coptic woman's Y-strap leather sandal dating from c. sixth century CE.

THE WORLD'S FIRST CONCEALED SHOE?

In 2013 seven leather shoes (three pairs and one single) were found deposited in a jar in an Egyptian temple at Luxor. The shoe-filled jar had been 'deliberately placed in a small space between two mudbrick walls,' according to the archaeologist Angelo Sesana in a report that was published in the journal *Memnoniaw*. While the temple itself predates the shoes by more than one thousand years, the shoes are thought to be some two thousand years old and foreign made. There is some discussion as to whether the shoes are the world's earliest example of a 'concealed' find (see pp. 120–1).

RIGHT: A Roman leather shoe made during the second century CE. The shoe's upper has a pattern of dots punched through the leather, allowing the foot to breathe. The shoe fastens with interlocking loops and has a hobnailed sole to prevent wear.

LEFT: An Egyptian man's right foot woven-straw sandal, c. nineteenth century BCE. With a distinct, pointed toe, the sandal has a hole through which a strap could run between the first and second toes. There is no strap remaining, but traces of it can be seen at the waist edges and there is an impression of it right across the width. The sandal has no heel and is flat-soled.

19

CRISPIN AND CRISPIANUS
PATRON SAINTS OF SHOEMAKERS

Two brothers, Crispin and Crispianus, have long been held as the patron saints of tanners, cobblers and leather workers, their feast day traditionally being celebrated annually on 25 October. In past times, this day would have been a shoemakers' holiday during which boot- and shoemakers closed their shops. In London, they were even known to hold a procession to and from church.

The tradition dates back to medieval Europe and two very different accounts of their story. A French version claims that the brothers came from a wealthy Roman family living in 287 CE. Having converted to Christianity, the men learned the craft of shoemaking to earn a living. Under threat of religious persecution, they fled to the ancient town of Soissons in northern France, but were nevertheless found, arrested and tortured. Despite being flung into a river with millstones tied around their necks, the men did not drown. The brothers were plunged into boiling lead and then into boiling oil but still did not die. Eventually their persecutors cut off their heads – and their martyrdom was sealed.

An English version of the story recounts that the brothers were sons of the Queen of Kent. As followers of Christianity, they fled to Faversham in disguise in order to escape persecution. It was here that they were apprenticed as shoemakers to a man called Robards. One day Crispin was sent to Canterbury with shoes for the Roman emperor's daughter, Ursula. Inevitably, the two fell in love and secretly married. Meanwhile Crispianus became a soldier in the Roman army and was honoured by the emperor. On hearing that the two brothers were princes, he approved of the marriage between Crispin and Ursula. When the brothers died they were buried in Faversham.

The Battle of Agincourt was fought on St Crispian's Day (25 October 1415). William Shakespeare draws attention to the fact in his play *Henry V* (Act IV Scene iii, 18–67):

This day is called the feast of Crispian.
He that outlives this day, and comes home safe,
Will stand a tip-toe when this day is named,
And rouse him at the name of Crispian…

And Crispin Crispian shall ne'er go by,
From this day to the ending of the world,
But we in it shall be remembered;
We few, we happy few, we band of brothers…

ABOVE: An engraved glass panel of St Crispin and St Crispianus, designed and created by John Hutton, 1962.

ABOVE: *The Martyrdom of Saints Crispin and Crispianus*, by Aert van den Bossche, 1494, and currently held at the National Museum of Warsaw, Poland. The two brothers suffered terrible beatings. They had their toenails removed, were flayed, pushed off a cliff and boiled alive! Today the brothers are the patron saints of such craftsmen as cobblers, lace makers, saddlers, glove makers and weavers.

2

FROM THE MIDDLE AGES TO THE RENAISSANCE

1200 TO THE 1580s

After the fall of the Roman Empire in 476 CE, Western Europe descended into a period of widespread instability, with various Germanic tribes – Huns, Goths and Vandals among them – terrorizing local populations as they sought to define new kingdoms. Charlemagne established the Holy Roman Empire in Central Europe in 800 and the Normans defeated the Anglo-Saxons to gain hold of England in 1066. By 1200 crusades had opened up the East to Western Europe, and trade routes to the Far East were set up.

By the turn of the first millennium, the vast majority of people were engaged in a feudal system of landowners and serfs, the latter farming the former's land. Agriculture began to boom from around 1100 and a number of trades were established, with blacksmiths, coopers and carpenters among them. Nevertheless the vast majority of Europe's wealth lay in the hands of the very few. Towns and cities grew in number, initially in ports, but gradually throughout Europe, attracting rural inhabitants seeking better lives. Much of this period was dominated by the Hundred Years' War (1337–1453), a series of conflicts between the English and French over the claim to the French throne, which culminated in a victory for France.

A MATTER OF SOCIAL STANDING

Shoes were status symbols. Few luxury goods were available and textiles for clothing, hangings and furnishings were prohibitively expensive. The shoes one wore and the textiles on show in the home proved an effective way of revealing wealth, status and power. They were investment pieces to be displayed at every opportunity, and while the many manuscripts of the day suggest that even the poorest people wore shoes, the elaborate versions were only available to those who could afford them. They also had to be new, of course, rather than simply repaired or remodelled and bought second-hand.

FROM THE LONG TO THE HIGH TO THE WIDE

Medieval shoes that have survived this period reflect the European fashions of the day: the long-toed poulaine and wide-toed footbags. They also reveal the decorative slashes, cuts and perforations that would have featured on the most expensive pairs of shoes. Unfortunately additional materials used for decoration, such as silks and velvets, have long since perished – in the right conditions, leather can last much longer than textiles. But it is still possible to imagine the range of footwear when partnered with contemporary accounts and images.

With the exception of the chopine, shoes had flat soles, while fastenings ranged from latchets and toggles to laces and small buckles. Low-cut shoes were worn throughout the fourteenth century with ankle boots popular before and after. Hose, a covering for the legs, were a particular feature of this period. Sewn from two pieces of woven fabric, versions in the mid-twelfth century even had leather soles to give the appearance that no shoes were being worn at all.

TECHNICAL DEVELOPMENTS

Construction methods included the invention of the rand in the middle of the twelfth century. A narrow strip of leather sewn between the upper and sole of the shoe, the rand made shoes a little more watertight. In the early thirteenth century, a shaped or waisted sole (the waist being the narrow part under the arch of the foot) appeared, which meant that shoes could now be made with left and right versions. Such an innovation probably increased the comfort of wearing shoes, too.

Most footwear from this period used goat, calf and deer hides, tanned using vegetable dyes. Decorative elements included appliqué work and embroidery, openwork decoration and cut-out patterns. An effigy of Edward III in Westminster Abbey, London, wears decorated shoes – probably in imitation of embroidery – with panels of leaves separated by a stylized cross.

STRUCTURING THE INDUSTRY

The shoemaking profession was well established in Europe by the Middle Ages. Every major town had at least one shoemaker producing high-quality, made-to-measure footwear for those who could afford it and a range of shoes in standard sizes for those who couldn't.

As was common with many trades at the time, shoe-related tradesmen and craftsmen banded together to form guilds in order to protect their common interests and maintain high standards of craftsmanship. Among the guilds established in England was the Guild of Cordwainers (1272) in London. The name cordwainer was taken from a corruption of Cordoba, the town in Spain famous for its cordwain (alum-tanned goatskin). Tanned using processes known only by the Moors, these soft leathers were the fashionable material for shoe uppers throughout the period.

Cordwainer became the preferred term for a craftsman who used such leather to fashion new shoes – as opposed to a cobbler, who traditionally dealt in second-hand shoes. While shoes needing repairs were returned to a cordwainer, a cobbler bought up old shoes and reconditioned them. The division of their respective roles was clear. In 1409 a ruling prohibited cobblers from using new leather for soles and quarters (the sides of a shoe upper), but allowed them to 'clout old boots and shoes with new leather upon the old soles, before or behind' (Mander, 1931). Clouting is defined as the patching of cloth or leather for mending.

Shoemakers were also organized in guilds in Italy. One of the oldest was L'Arte dei Calegheri, founded in Venice in 1268. The first school for training shoemakers had been established as early as 1144 in Bologna. Medieval Italian shoemakers grouped together depending on the type of shoe they made. In Venice those who made shoes and sandals were considered differently from those making low-quality shoes, or those who repaired them. Rights and privileges were granted to shoemakers who belonged to these groups. Shoemakers also banded together to protect their interests through guilds in other European countries, such as France and Spain.

It would be another five hundred years or so before shoemakers became established in North America. According to American shoemaker and historian Al Saguto, 'The first English shoemakers arrived at Jamestown in

LEFT: *The Shoemaker* by David Teniers the Younger, c. 1650, depicts a shoemaker in his workshop. Shoemaking was often a lonely occupation and there is a long tradition of shoemakers keeping birds for company. In the painting, the shoemaker sits on a stool with his tools on a nearby bench. Some of the tools of the trade can be seen, including the shoemaker's knife and the stirrup (leather strap) that was used to hold a boot or shoe firmly on the knee when lasting and sewing. The block under the shoemaker's foot raises up his knee to a more convenient height for working.

1610…John Rolf (married Pocahontas) noted that shoemaking and tanning were thriving in Virginia by 1616.' Not long after, he continues, 'the first Pilgrim settlers landed in Massachusetts. The first shoemakers who followed the trade there arrived in 1629.'

THE TURNSHOE
By the beginning of the Middle Ages the most common form of shoemaking was 'turnshoe' construction. The upper was lasted (pulled into shape over a mould called a last) inside out and stitched onto the sole (also reversed). The whole construction was then turned right-side out, leaving the sole seam concealed on the inside. As a method of construction, it didn't lend itself well to mass production and so was finally replaced by the welted shoe, in which the upper and insole were sewn to the welt – a narrow piece of leather – and stitched to the sole. No seam is visible inside. The turnshoe method of construction is still in use today for making slippers and ballet shoes.

RIGHT: *The Shoemaker* by Jost Amman in Hans Sachs's *The Book of Trades* (Nuremberg, 1568). The man seated to the left is stitching the welt using a double-ended thread. In front of him, on the bench, are his thread and moon knife. Traditionally, there are two kinds of knives used for cutting leather. The half-moon knife, depicted in Egyptian paintings of 1450 BCE and Greek carvings of around 550 BCE, and a curved-bladed handknife – arched to aid paring and trimming – also known as the moon knife, which became the blade of choice by the late medieval period.

THE LONG

One of the most distinctive and intriguing shoe styles of the medieval period was the poulaine, also known as the pike or Crakow. A low-cut, flat-soled, slip-on shoe – sometimes fastened with a side lace or toggle – the poulaine's distinctive feature was its very pronounced, pointed toe. In his great chronicle of the eleventh and twelfth centuries, *Histora Ecclesiastica*, Oderic Vitalis called such shoes 'scorpion tails'.

The poulaine is thought to have originated in Krakow, Poland, one of the most important cultural centres in Europe at the time. The style was first seen in Poland in 1340 and it enjoyed popularity throughout much of Europe until around 1475. While France and England were quick to adopt the style, Amsterdam, in the Netherlands was not a commercial centre until the late fifteenth century, and adopted them later. By 1500 the style had all but disappeared.

Worn across the social classes, poulaines favoured by working men and women had shorter toes for practical reasons, while the wealthy opted for more exaggerated, longer-toed versions. Not only were they status symbols, but shoes with longer toes carried a suggestion of the wearer's masculinity. Echoes of this can be seen in the winklepicker of the 1950s (see pp. 198–9) and Vivienne Westwood's penis shoe of 1995.

The longest versions were expensive and difficult to make, with the extra leather needed for the toe stitched straight through from one side to the other. The toes were often stuffed with moss to provide a degree of rigidity should they be trodden on and squashed. They could even be manipulated to raise them off the ground at a slight angle in order to aid walking. Certainly, the tips of poulaines that have survived show very little wear.

Claims have been made that, to make the shoes easier to walk in, a length of cord or chain was attached between the toe of the shoe and the wearer's waistband or kneeband. However several written sources including the late fourteenth-century *Eulogium Historiarium* and that written by John Stow in 1598 appear to have been misread, and there is no evidence that such a thing occurred. One of the world's leading shoe historians, June Swann, states that, 'In spite of searching primary sources for confirmation of this for over fifty years, I have found nothing…What is certain is that the word "poulaine" was also used for leg armour and a reference *c.* 1390 mentions "grevez, with polaynez picked thereto…about his knees knegged with knots of gold"'.

COURTING CONTROVERSY

Of course such a style invited comment and ridicule from all levels of society. William Langland in his narrative poem *Piers Plowman* of *c.* 1377 describes 'Vain priests, in the company of the anti-Christ wearing pyked shoes'.

More stringent reactions came from other quarters. Several attempts sought to put an end to the ridiculously long toes. Sumptuary laws were passed in England in 1368 and 1464, capping the toe to 5 cm (2 in). The French passed similar laws in 1422 and the Pope in 1362 and 1468. Such laws attempted to restrict the sumptuousness of dress in order to curb extravagance, to protect fortunes and to define necessary and appropriate distinctions between the different strata of society.

LEFT: Long, pointed toes are not confined to the Western world. The elaborate gold embroidery and upturned toes of these mojaris reflect the impact of the Mogul court, whose influence dominated India from the sixteenth to the eighteenth century. The upturned toes indicate status.

BELOW: This poulaine, dating from around 1350–1400, is one of a large group of shoes recovered from archaeological excavations at Baynard's Castle on the north bank of the River Thames, London (now Queen Victoria Street). It is thought that these shoes came from wealthy households, since few of them show any signs of repair. A number may even have come from the Royal Wardrobe, which lay to the north of the excavation site.

THE HIGH

An extraordinary style to emerge during the Middle Ages was the sky-scraping chopine. Reaching heights up to 45 cm (18 in), the chopine originated as a form of overshoe, which was then modified for wear on its own. Although some consider the style to be the first shoe with a heel, technically it is a platform-soled shoe.

Chopines are thought to have originated in fifteenth-century Venice, where they were long associated with prostitutes. The idea was that the elevated shoes raised them above the heads of rivals when catching the eye of a prospective client. The style was subsequently adopted by Venetian aristocracy and gradually filtered through to the rest of Italy and throughout much of Western Europe.

In reality, women across the social strata would have worn the style, although for different reasons. Not only did the prostitute gain height, but also a sensuous gait when walking. For the aristocrat, wearing shoes that rendered a woman practically immobile served as an indication of her social standing – not only could she afford expensive shoes of the highest quality, but such was her lifestyle that she didn't need to work and could therefore wear impractical shoes.

According to Elizabeth Semmelhack, shoe historian and curator at the Bata Shoe Museum in Toronto, Canada, the chopine 'played an important supporting role in the expression of opulence through dress, specifically in relation to the display of cloth'. Although the style existed in more modest heights, the tall versions were the most sought after. The wood or cork platforms (for lightness) were decorated with leather, brocades, velvets, cut-outs and slashing. So popular was the style in Spain that the country almost ran out of cork!

'What a prodigious affectation is that of chopines where our ladies imitated the Venetian and Persian ladies.'

Dr John Bulwer in his play *Anthropometamorphosis: Man Transformed or Artificial Changeling*, 2nd ed., 1653.

WAS THE CHOPINE PRACTICAL?

Inspiration for the style is said to have come from the towering wooden bath clogs that women wore in Turkish bathhouses to lift them above the wet, hot marble floors. They were practical in that they raised the wearer out of the wet, yet women walking in such towering footwear, inlaid with mother-of-pearl, were unstable and inelegant. Some reports indicate that women needed the support of servants to move around, but in his dancing manual, *Nobilta di Dame* (1600), Fabrito Caroso wrote that, with care, a woman could 'move with grace, seemliness and beauty'.

The chopine held some favour in the rest of Western Europe, but it was in Venice that the shoe's popularity reached heady heights. Although not adopted in England, when Lady Jane Grey was presented at court in 1553, she received a pair of chopines to wear. A description of this was made by Sir Baptist Spinola, a Genoese merchant living in Italy at the time: 'The new queen was mounted on very high chopines [clogs] to make her look much taller, which were concealed by her robes, as she is very small and short'.

As with poulaines, chopines met with a certain amount of criticism, particularly by the Church. A priest in Spain condemned the style as early as 1438.

LEFT: Stilted shoes known as 'kub kabs' or 'quabquabs' were worn by wealthy women in the Ottoman Empire as early as 1600. This pair is made from wood inlaid with mother-of-pearl and date from the late nineteenth century.

RIGHT: *Turkish Woman and Her Slave*, by Jean-Etienne Liotard, eighteenth century. The artist was an avid traveller, recording through his illustrations the individuals and wonders he saw. This Turkish woman wears slip-on shoes with her 'kub kabs', while her servant is barefoot (though her feet are painted with henna).

THE WIDE

Out went the long-toed poulaine (see pp. 28–9) and in came the footbag, so called because wearing the shoe was likened to putting your foot into a bag. It was also known as the cow's mouth, the hornbill, the platypus or the bear paw. The complete opposite of the poulaine in terms of shape, the footbag was flat-soled but had a broad toe. It could be a simple slip-on shoe or, alternately, have a bar strap across the foot or be fastened with a small buckle.

Poulaines had all but disappeared by 1500 and, in their place, merchant classes across Europe were beginning to enjoy an altogether wider, more relaxed style. This was a time of great political, intellectual and social change in Europe that coincided with an increase in both the presence and influence of a rich and powerful bourgeoisie. Naturally, the fashions of the day reflected this. The vertical lines of the Gothic, manifested in the long toe of the poulaine, gave way to the horizontal lines so evident in the square, boxed, padded shoulders and wide shoes that were typified by the English King, Henry VIII (r. 1509–47). Such dress emphasized power, wealth and sheer presence.

Sometimes the toes of footbags were padded with straw, wool or moss – anything that might create an even greater bulbous effect, which was every bit as suggestive as the exaggerated toe of the poulaine. François Rabelais mentions the style in his novel, *The Life of Gargantua and of Pantagruel*: 'They were shoes as round as basins'. And when it came down to width, the soles of some shoes during Henry's reign reached an incredible 17 cm (6½ in). As in the case of the poulaine, sumptuary laws were passed in an attempt to curb such excesses.

SURFACE DECORATION

Footbags worn by the working classes were relatively simple. Tudor shoes excavated in the City of London are of brown leather turned black with age and have flat soles. Most are slip-ons, and there are some that fasten with a small buckle.

Climbing up the social ladder, more elaborate styles were available to those who could afford them. At a time when Henry VIII was vying for fashion supremacy with the French King, Francis I, this sartorial competition manifested most keenly in decorative details and surface embellishments. Slashed decoration – the mainstay of doublets during this period – was introduced to footwear in around 1514 and was popular in Germany as well as England. Leather vamps (the front part of a shoe upper that covers the toes and

LEFT: This portrait of King Henry VIII, 1537–62, shows the English monarch adopting a characteristic stance. The overall impression sums up the bulky, square look that epitomized wealth and status throughout medieval Europe, and which is echoed in the width of Henry's shoes. The artist of this painting is unknown, although the work is derived from the Whitehall mural, painted by Hans Holbein in 1537.

part of the instep) might be slashed horizontally, vertically or diagonally to reveal flashes of sumptuously coloured silk lining beneath the surface. Toes varied in shape and included such styles as the square toe, the horned toe and the hammerhead. Quite literally resembling the end of a hammer, this last style had protrusions sticking out of either side at the end of the toe. Women's footbags were similar in style to those of the men, although less extravagant.

NEW CONSTRUCTION METHODS

By the end of the fifteenth century the typical turnshoe construction of the period was giving way to the welted shoe (see p. 28). At the time, low-vamped shoes had two side pieces that met together at the back. The pieces were called 'quarters' since the shoemaker used four of them to make each pair of shoes.

BELOW: This sixteenth-century leather footbag was discovered during archaeological excavations in London. The simplicity of its design suggests the shoe would have been worn by an ordinary citizen.

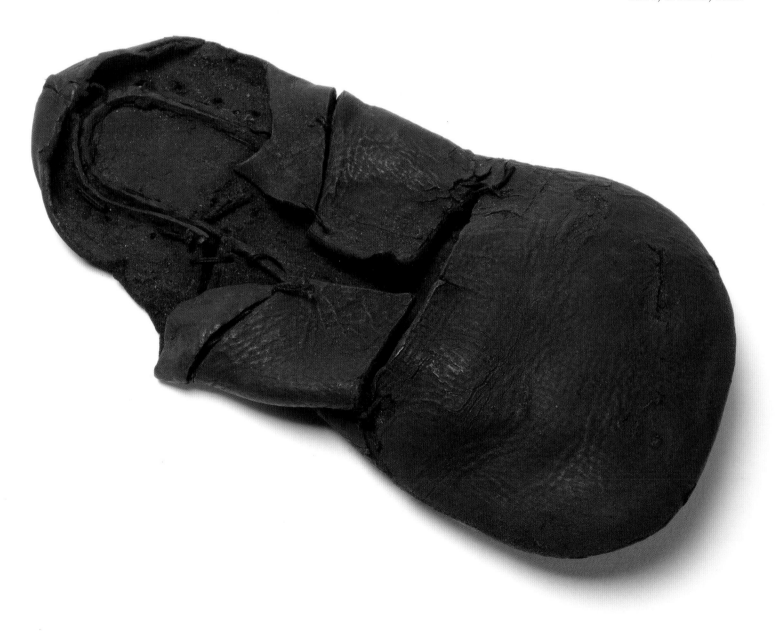

SHOE SIZES

A degree of mystery surrounds early shoe sizing. Shoemakers' marks have been found on early shoes but, frustratingly, each seems to follow its own unique system. It could be that shoemakers protected their interests in this way – keeping a client's shoe size a closely guarded secret might prevent him or her from straying.

ESTABLISHING A SYSTEM

The English system for measuring foot length dates back to 1324. At the time, King Edward II decreed that three barleycorns laid end to end were the equivalent of 2.5 cm (one inch). It happened that thirty-six barleycorns equalled the length of an average man's foot and so 30 cm (twelve inches) counted as one 'foot'.

The longest foot at the time measured thirty-nine barleycorns or 33 cm (thirteen inches), and this became a Size 13. Initially, smaller sizes were graded down by 0.75 cm (one third of an inch). Eventually, however, this system proved too crude for any great accuracy and so half sizes

were introduced as well. This early introduction of a sizing system would imply that, even in the fourteenth century, shoes were available as ready-mades as well as bespoke.

Sizes were standard in Britain by 1885, with the United States following two years later. In addition to half sizes, a range of shoe widths ensured that one could get a good fit without the expense of custom-made footwear. The sizing system used in the United States is similar to that in the United Kingdom, but has a different starting point. While the first UK size is 0, the US equivalent is 1, and so US shoes are one and one-half sizes larger than their British counterparts.

An early system of sizing in France, widespread by Napoleonic times, used the length of a Parisian stitch as its base unit, which was ⅔ cm (¼ in). Today, the system is referred to as Paris point and is the standard across continental Europe. The shoe size is the length of the last used to make it, expressed in Paris point. Since one Paris point measures ⅔ cm (¼ in), the calculation is made thus: length of last in centimetres multiplied by two over three.

LEFT: A sixteenth-century English woodcut entitled *The Shoemaker*. It shows the shoemaker at work, sewing a shoe held in place firmly on his knee with the aid of a leather stirrup, which is looped over the shoe and under his foot.

ABOVE: An engraving from Paul Lacroix's *Science and Literature in the Middle Ages and the Renaissance* (1878), entitled *The Shoemaker Fitting a Shoe*. The engraving is a direct copy of one of ninety-six such carvings that feature on the Misericordia Stalls in the choir of Rouen Cathedral, France, and which depict professions of the fifteenth century.

PATTENS
STILTS FOR RAINY DAYS

It's unlikely that medieval shoes were all that waterproof. Certainly wearers would have experienced difficulties walking through wet, muddy or snowy streets in shoes with flat soles. At the time, the most practical response came with the development of the patten.

The first reference to patten makers in Britain occurs in 1216. There is also a reference to women wearing stilts in the Luttrell Psalter of c. 1320–40. Pattens were also worn in many north European countries.

The patten was a wooden, foot-shaped platform. Some versions involved a solid wooden wedge from toe to heel, while others had stilts at the toe and heel ends. Either way, pattens could raise the wearer 5 cm (2 in) off the ground. Research by Rowena Gail on medieval pattens excavated in London shows that the common types of wood were alder, willow and poplar. Alder is resilient to wet conditions and, while not the longest lasting of woods, is easy to work with. It has long been the choice for the English clog industry (see pp. 136–7). Poplar and willow are tough and not prone to splintering. In mainland Europe clogs and pattens were made from close-grained woods such as walnut, plane or elm. They too came in different styles with higher or lower stilts. When it came to shape, it was common for pattens to echo the popular shoe styles of the day – the poulaine, for example (see pp. 28–9).

WEARING PATTENS

The idea was to strap a pair of pattens in place over regular shoes. Leather straps were nailed to the pattens for this purpose, initially reaching across the instep but also, by the late fourteenth century, around the heel for a more secure fit. Usually made from one solid piece of wood, a patten had no flexibility and must have been difficult to walk in. Later, hinged versions may well have been introduced to deal specifically with this problem.

Early pattens that have survived show signs of decoration, including painted designs, stitching and embossed motifs. This suggests that pattens were first worn by the upper classes in order to protect their finer shoes from inclement conditions. However, by the fifteenth century everyone was using them. Versions existed that were made from foot-shaped layers of thick cowhide stitched together.

ABOVE: The *Arnolfini Portrait* by Jan Van Ecyk, 1434, represents the Italian merchant Giovanni di Nicolao Arnolfini and his wife in their Flemish home. The portrait, which currently hangs in the National Gallery, London, features several items that indicate the merchant status of its subjects, not least the pair of pattens placed casually in the foreground.

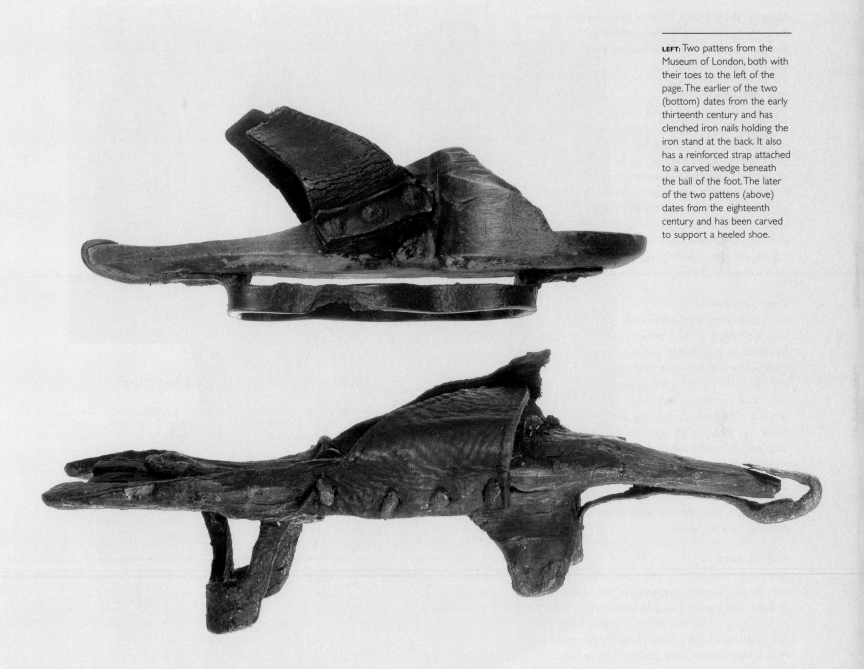

LEFT: Two pattens from the Museum of London, both with their toes to the left of the page. The earlier of the two (bottom) dates from the early thirteenth century and has clenched iron nails holding the iron stand at the back. It also has a reinforced strap attached to a carved wedge beneath the ball of the foot. The later of the two pattens (above) dates from the eighteenth century and has been carved to support a heeled shoe.

3

EUROPEAN RENAISSANCE

1590s TO THE 1650s

A CULTURAL SHIFT

The Renaissance that had started in Italy, primarily Florence, towards the end of the fifteenth century, rapidly gained ground throughout Europe. This rebirth – a surge in the desire for knowledge and a reacquaintance with the work of ancient Greek and Roman scholars – coincided with emerging technologies and new scientific discoveries, elevating Western Europe to new cultural heights. Europe's elite was expanding, too, and included the relatively new merchant classes who were benefiting from the spoils of increased trade. Demands for the most beautiful and expensive silks, satins, velvets and jewels were on the rise in a bid to satisfy the needs of the new bourgeoisie.

EUROPEAN TRENDS

Through his accession to the Spanish throne in 1516, the Austrian Hapsburg King Charles I united Spain with the Holy Roman Empire, creating a vast realm that included much of Western Europe as well as parts of America following the discovery of the New World. Spain's power was unrivalled, not only politically, but also in terms of trade, since it had control of long-established ports in Italy and the Netherlands as well as those in Spain itself. The union of the Spanish and English monarchies through the marriages of Henry VIII to Catherine of Aragon and his daughter, Mary Tudor, to King Philip of Spain, also did much to increase the influence of Spain. The Spanish exhibited a passion for dark, quite sombre and severe clothing, which the English also found appealing. Black was a popular colour and there were a number of reasons for this. First and foremost, it was a difficult colour to achieve successfully through dyeing and this made it prohibitively expensive to all but the wealthiest. Secondly, it provided the best background on which to display dazzling precious stones and pearls. The English also adopted the Spanish fashion for cloaks and a sleeveless leather jerkin. Such jerkins were worn with leather boots, gloves and a hat to complete the look.

NEW HEIGHTS OF FASHION

It was during this period that the first heels with distinct arches began to emerge. A far cry from the chopines of the previous century, the heels seen from the late 1500s onwards were modest (in comparison, at least) at 7.5 cm (2–3 in) and more shapely. Shoemakers faced a number of challenges in adding heels to their shoes – not least their tendency to snap off under the weight of their wearer – but the style endured and went on to dominate shoe fashions for both men and women for at least the next hundred years. Another development from the period was that of latchet ties, which enabled shoemakers to embellish their designs with all manner of flamboyant ribbons, ties and roses, much to the delight of their wealthy patrons.

PURITAN VALUES

While velvet initially proved a very popular material for shoes during this period fashions began to change during the mid-seventeenth century, with leather shoes becoming more prominent. The move coincided with social tensions, in England at least, that followed the Civil War of 1642.

The sumptuous and lavish shoe styles that characterized the first half of the seventeenth century contrasted starkly with more sober styles and colours that emerged during the second half, and which the Puritans favoured and exported to the early settlements of New England. The first shoemakers to arrive in America went to Jamestown, Virginia, the first permanent English settlement established in 1607. The styles they crafted would have reflected those made back in England: open- or closed-sided, leather, latchet-style shoes, depending on one's wealth.

THE FIRST HEELS

The first shoe with a distinct heel emerged during the last quarter of the sixteenth century. The style was slow to gain favour and it wasn't until the first quarter of the seventeenth century that such shoes became widespread, with heels reaching heights of 7.5 cm (2 to 3 in).

The origins of the heel are much debated. On the one hand, it would seem a natural progression from the medieval platform chopine (see pp. 30–1). Now modified, the heel provided a practical, lightweight and less cumbersome alternative to the chopine and the wedged shoes of previous decades. However, senior curator at the Bata Shoe Museum in Toronto, Canada, Elizabeth Semmelhack, believes that the heel 'was not a European invention nor was it a new form of footwear. Heels had been worn by Near Eastern men for centuries as a form of equestrian footwear, designed to secure the foot in the stirrup while riding.'

It is true that diplomats and trade missions might have related tales of heeled shoes from their travels. And printed works, such as Flemish painter Pieter Coecke van Aelst's widely read *Moeurs et fachons de faires des Turck* (*Customs and Fashions of the Turks*), published in the sixteenth century, might also have influenced the evolution of the heel in Europe. Was the chopine a source of inspiration for the heel? Semmelhack raises an interesting point concerning whether the 'enthusiastic adoption of the heel by upper-class men' really did evolve from 'such a gendered, and widely ridiculed, form of footwear as the chopine.'

Elizabeth I can be seen wearing what look like wedge-heeled shoes in two images: one by Will Rogers, 1593–5, and the other by an unknown artist in *c.* 1599. These wedge-heeled shoes look like pantofles, and indeed Elizabeth I had many pairs of such footwear.

Whatever the origins of the heel, the first written reference to heels was recorded by clothing historian Janet Arnold in *Queen Elizabeth's Wardrobe Unlock'd*. Arnold records, from a list dated 1595, 'a payre of spanyshe lether shoes with highe heels and arches' and in 1598, pantobles with 'arches and high heels.'

STRAIGHTS

Making shoes with distinct and separate heels posed a problem for shoemakers when it came to producing pairs with left and right versions. The procedure was fairly simple for flat-soled shoes, particularly when sole waists became more pronounced; the shoemaker simply drew around the foot. Adding a heel posed problems in making mirror-image lasts with heels, and creating the right balance when worn. In response, shoemakers abandoned the waisted sole altogether and made both shoes in a pair identical – they called them 'straights'. The shoes became moulded into left and right versions through wear.

Both men and women wore shoes with heels, with the heel either carved from solid wood and covered with leather or textile or made from stacked leather pieces. The addition of a heel, particularly on women's shoes, often led to weak arches where the heel attached to the shoe. To counter this, shoemakers ran leather the entire length of a sole and down the heel breast to prevent the heel snapping under the weight of the wearer.

BELOW: Women's silk brocade latchet-tie shoe. A ribbon would have passed through the holes in the small latchets, to help keep the shoe on. Late seventeenth century.

RIGHT: *The Merchant of Venice*, by Sir James D Linton, *c.* sixteenth century. This Venetian merchant wears a gown lined with ermine, striped stockings and has a feather in his cap. His white leather shoes are heeled and each is embellished with an elaborate red rose.

LATCHET-TIE SHOES AND MULES

Introduced in 1610, the square-toed shoe dominated shoe fashions in Europe for much of the seventeenth century. In fact, the style was so closely associated with men's shoes that when fashions changed in the next century, an unfashionable man was called 'old square toes'.

LATCHET TIES

Up until this point a narrower shoe with blunted (yet still pointed) toe and increased sole thickness had been fashionable. Slip-on shoes also fell out of favour during this period with both men and women. Instead, there was a

preference for latchet-tie shoes with high tongues. Typical examples had two short latchets that almost met across the instep, with a tongue beneath. Laces and ribbon ties threaded through holes in the latchets before tying.

By the time King James I came to power in England in 1603, this style was prevalent, though changes were starting to evolve. Shoemakers began to cut away the quarters to leave openings at the sides, and these became increasingly larger. Men and women wore similar styles in a rather modern unisex manner. Shoes were generally light in colour, with white proving most popular for formalwear.

BELOW: This pair of women's silver and blue brocade latchet shoes, c. 1680, are typical of those seen in wealthy European society. Features include the French Louis heel – here at 6 cm (2½ in) tall – covered in brocade.

POM-POM MULES

The mule is prevalent in other parts of the world. These pom-pom mules – called *tauranwari jutti* – are from Pakistan, where the jutti has been worn since the early sixteenth century. This pair, dating from 1970, is made from leather and wool and originates from the Sindh province. They are suited to the hilly sandy environment: the pom-poms cushion the feet at the front, while the narrow backs make it easy to flick out trapped sand.

LEFT: An elegant pair of men's pale blue, now faded, satin mules, c. 1620–30. They have long, square, duckbill toes and a vamp trimmed with silver braid. The heels are low at 3.5 cm (1½ in).

MULES

The mule also became a popular style of footwear for both men and women during the seventeenth century. A mule was a backless shoe or slipper with or without a heel, and some wonderful examples exist. Worn as indoor shoes, they were not subject to such vigorous wear and so considerably more pairs have survived, and in better condition. Later, when this style came into fashion in the United States, mules were known as slides. Mules were a sign of wealth – an indication that one could afford to have a separate pair of shoes for indoors. Such beautiful shoes were very expensive and would certainly not have stood up to outdoor wear. Typically, mules had low, covered heels and were often embroidered in metal thread. A range of toe shapes existed, including a forked toe (a squared toe with slightly elongated corner points) that was more subtle than versions seen in the sixteenth century.

SLAP SOLES

The advent of the heel made medieval pattens (see pp. 36–7) redundant, yet heels fared little better in wet and muddy conditions should inclement weather prevail. Worse still, the newly adopted heel was prone to sinking into soft ground, which only exacerbated the problem. In response, some men began to wear their high-heeled shoes slipped into mules.

The effect was to spread the weight of the wearer and so prevent sinking. A print by Frenchman Jacques Callot, *La Noblesse* (1624), shows a man so equipped. Although they look good, the combination must have been quite difficult to keep on one's feet. The remedy? To combine the heel and the mule in to a single style: the 'slap sole' had been born. No references to the exact origins of these shoes has been found to date, but it is known that they were worn in Italy and other European countries.

AN INNOVATIVE CONSTRUCTION

In a slap sole, the sole extends the entire length of the shoe – even under the high heel. It is not attached to the heel, however. When walking, therefore, the sole slaps against the heel with quite a clatter – hence the name of the shoe. The style was better at keeping footwear on the foot, but in reality it did not prevent any serious sinking. Further, why the sole was not attached to the heel is open to question. Could it be simply that the wearer rather liked the slapping noise that accompanied him when making an entrance?

Originally worn by men, the slap sole was adopted by women as a fashion accessory by the second half of the seventeenth century. In such cases, it was often worn indoors. Certainly, many surviving examples show little sign of outdoor wear, and some even have felt attached to the soles in order to deaden the noise for indoor use – proof, perhaps, that a grand entrance was not always appreciated.

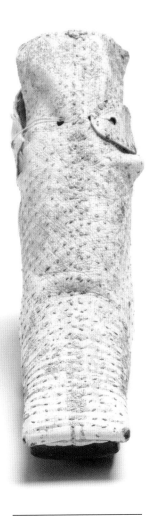

LEFT AND ABOVE: A woman's white leather, slap-sole shoe, 1625–40s. It has a high instep with latchets for lacings over and through the tongue, a duckbill toe and a 7.5 cm (3 in) covered heel. The leather slap sole extends under the heel but is not attached to it. The shoe was originally covered with bands of narrow silk braid, and the stitching lines can still be seen.

THE SHOE ROSE

Portraiture from the Renaissance shows Europe's most wealthy dressed in beautiful clothes made from the finest fabrics. Any feet visible in such images are also clad in stunning shoes adorned with elaborate decorations and embellishments. As early as 1588, the English pamphleteer Philip Stubbs, in his *Anatomie of Abuses*, remarked that shoes were 'stitched with silk and embroidered with gold and silver all over the foot with gew-gaws innumerable.'

At their simplest, shoes had ribbon ties threaded through small holes in their latchets and fastened across the instep, often in contrasting colours. Steadily the ribbons grew in size to become features in their own right, along with large bows, rosettes and spangles decorated with drop pearls. Court roses of ribbons twisted into a rosette or gathered into a large, ruffled puff became all the rage among the English nobility, as can be seen in the portrait of Lady Dorothy Cary by William Larkin, *c.* 1614. She wears white leather, open-sided shoes with latchet ties covered by gold roses with green centres.

AN ENGLISH FASHION
Shoe roses and ribbon embellishments could be found on upper-class footwear throughout Europe, though it was a dominant fashion in England. There is a portrait of the Infante Don Carlos by Diego Velázquez, 1628, which shows him wearing small black shoe roses. Similar embellishments appear in a miniature of Richard Sackville, 3rd Earl of Dorset, painted in 1616 by Isaac Oliver. Here, the beautiful shoes have open sides and huge golden roses. The miniature also expresses the importance not just of the shoes, but of the stockings. Sackville's are an elaborate example, and a colourful part of the overall look. Such decoration, often edged with metallic thread, was very expensive. Sackville, who spent nearly all of his fortune on clothes, counted his shoe roses as separate, special items in his wardrobe – and especially his shoes roses made of gold lace (see quote).

It was not unusual during this period for shoes to be decorated in one design, stockings in another and doublet in a third. The result, quite often, was a cacophony of colour, pattern and conspicuous wealth. John Webster, in his tragicomedy of 1623, *The Devil's Lawcase*, refers to

'overblown roses to hide your gouty ankles,' while Ben Johnson's play *The Devil Is an Ass* (first performed in 1616 and published in 1631) declared that shoe roses were 'big enough to hide a cloven hoof'.

Beneath these amazing roses the shoes themselves were pinked (the edge finished with a notched or sawtooth design) or decorated with slashes. On several shoes that survive from this period, the paired holes for attaching the decorative rose are clearly evident.

'59 item one paire of roses edged with gold and silver lace and 110 item one paire of greene roses edged with gold lace.'

'An Inventorie of the rich wearing Apparrell of the right honorable Richard Earle of Dorset', 1617.

BELOW: A pair of woman's ivory satin mules, embroidered with a flower design in coloured silks, silver thread and sequins, 1640–59. The mules are straights, meaning that there is not a left and a right version, but both are the same. They have a square, slightly overhanging toe and a 4.5 cm (1¾ in) covered heel.

SHOESTRINGS
A BRIEF HISTORY OF THE SHOELACE

Shoelaces have featured on shoes for a very long time. Romans wore shoes with long leather laces reaching up to their knees. Shoes in medieval times were such that extensive lacing was not necessary, yet they would have had just enough to help keep the shoe on.

During the early seventeenth century, the ribbon became fashionable in Europe with both men and women wearing latchet-tie shoes (see p. 46). This method of lacing a shoe was probably confined to the wealthy, as a ribbon would have been more expensive than leather and less hard-wearing. While the most moneyed, including courtiers, wore silk, rich landowners and merchants wore linen and working people used leather laces. Known as shoestrings at the time, rather than laces, some were tied into lovers' knots symbolizing love and friendship, while others lay concealed beneath spangles and extra decorations. The poet Robert Herrick wrote in his *Delights in Disorder* (1591–1674):

> In the tempestuous petticoat
> A careless shoestring, in whose tie
> I see a wild civility
> Do more bewitch me than when art
> Is too precise in every part.

Shoestrings appear to have had a double meaning. A writer in the *Tatler* magazine of the day scolds a shoemaker in London for having the temerity to expose in his shop window shoes sporting green laces and blue heels.

FUTURE DEVELOPMENTS
Popular until the mid-seventeenth century, laces, shoestrings and ribbons were superseded by buckles from the 1660s. It was not until the 1790s that shoestrings reappeared on men's footwear. Metal eyelets were patented in 1823 by Thomas Rogers, and lacing hooks in 1865. The woven braid lace appears during the later nineteenth century. From about 1890 to 1915 laces for fashion shoes were up to 2.5 cm

(1 in) wide and were usually made of silk (later artificial silk). More sensible shoelaces were made of cotton. The lace tag (called an aglet), originally a metal strip crimped at the ends of laces, appeared in the early nineteenth century.

SHOELACES TODAY
Shoelaces are ripe for customization. Many of the big sneaker brands today accessorize their sneakers with shoelace tags that have two holes through which the lace is passed. These are usually worn on one of the bars of lacing, ensuring that the motif or brand name on the tag is visible.

When it comes to threading a lace onto a shoe, there are many styles to choose from. They include over-under lacing, straight-bar lacing, ladder lacing and lattice lacing. As with the shoes themselves, it's a question of personal preference.

LEFT: In this portrayal of Dutch townsfolk from the *Münchener Bilderbogen*, c. 1680, this bourgeois couple is on their way to a masquerade. She wears a velvet muff, while he wears latchet-tie shoes with elaborate green ribbons.

ABOVE: This advertisement for shoelace manufacturers Faire Bros & Co. appeared in *The Boot and Shoe Trade Journal*, 14 May 1887.

RIGHT: Woman's green silk, latchet-tie shoe, c. 1675–1700. The upper is decorated with bands of braid and it has a needlepoint toe.

THE RISE OF THE BOOT

Towards the middle of the seventeenth century, European dress became less conspicuously extravagant. It showed greater refinement and a paring down of ornamentation. In England, men's footwear was dominated by military influences in the run up to the Civil War of 1642, and so it was that the boot became increasingly popular, and remained so until the 1690s.

A great source for contemporary images is the Flemish artist Anthony van Dyck. He painted many portraits of royalty and in particular Charles I. Some show the monarch in leather boots that come up to the knee with a turned-down top, a blunt toe and a low heel. The boots might also have sported a spur leather – a butterfly-shaped piece of hide at the front to which one could attach a spur to protect the soft leather. Under Charles I, these spur leathers became bigger and bigger. The boots often had an extended sole or galosh to prevent sinking in muddy terrain. Such boots were very expensive. Charles I had twenty pairs made between 1634 and 1635, each costing £24. In contrast a pair of shoes for a poor man was highlighted in Philip Massinger's play of 1632, *The City Madam*, in which 'a pair of shoes for the swineherd cost 16 pence' – more than three hundred times less.

EUROPEAN INTERPRETATIONS

Across Europe boots were made of very soft and supple leather that gave the appearance of wrinkled legs. They were soft enough to allow the tops to be turned over easily, while giving an easy fit around the leg. Worn by horse-mounted soliders, such boots became synonymous with Charles I's supporters, the Cavaliers. Some were made longer than necessary to allow the tops to be rolled over in a double fold, a cup shape (separately stitched on) or the iconic bucket shape. Bucket-topped boots were more robust than the Cavaliers' soft wrinkled boots. Made of thicker leather, they could sport tops that almost reached the ground.

Boots were available in varying shades of brown, black and grey. Buff leather and suede were materials used. To protect stockings from a boot's rough inner leather and the greasy or waxed surface of the exterior, footwear was lined with boot hose, often trimmed with lace, embroidery or a fringe. While men wore boots for both walking and riding, women tended to sport them for riding only.

LEFT: *Portrait of Sir Thomas Wharton* by Anthony van Dyck, 1639, and currently at the Hermitage, St Petersburg. Painted during van Dyck's time in England, his portrait of this English politician shows Wharton wearing cavalier boots with spur leathers.

Men's dark brown, blackish, buff leather boots, 1630–40s. The dark brown, shiny leather top has been stitched on to add contrast. These boots have blunt-pointed toes and 5 cm (2 in) stacked heels. Originally they would have had leather loops inside the top of the leg to help pull them on.

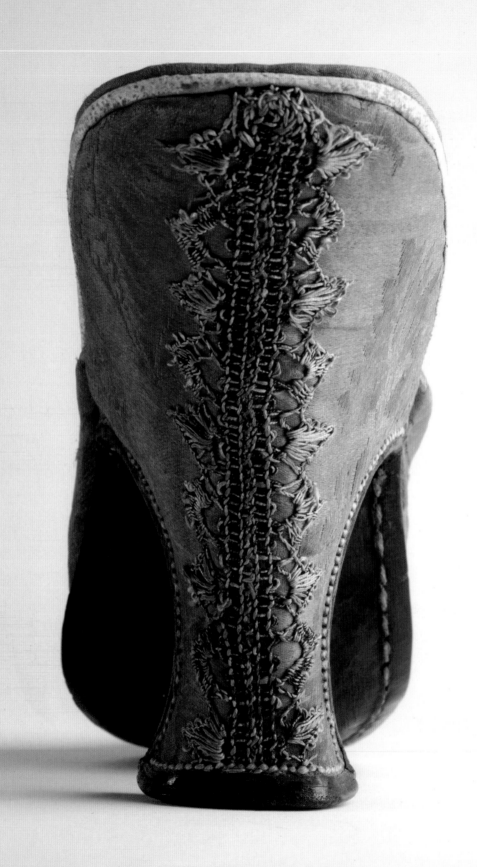

4

TOWARDS THE AGE OF REASON

1660s TO THE 1750s

FRENCH SUPREMACY

With Louis XIV wielding absolute power in France, the French dominated Europe from 1661. Embarking on a long reign of relative stability, the country dictated trends not only in politics, but in all areas of style and culture. Under the 'Sun King', France became not only the richest country in Europe – thanks to a shrewd economic policy that promoted domestic manufacturing and undermined foreign importation – but also the strongest, having amassed armed forces of some four hundred thousand men. This was the golden age of France and a time of great cultural supremacy, with the rest of Europe slavishly following the latest Gallic trends in style and etiquette.

Having undergone a period of political and cultural tumult following the end of the Civil War (1642–51), England also entered a new phase of prosperity once Charles II returned to power. As the seventeenth century came to a close and the eighteenth century steadily progressed, increased trade saw London become the largest city in the world and home to an increasingly prosperous middle class – all poised to see what the French nobility had on their feet.

TECHNICAL DEVELOPMENTS

The French King was the arbiter of good taste and personally established a trend for shoes with red heels, as portraits of the King from the time bear out. Heels with defined arches, which had emerged during the last quarter of the sixteenth century, continued to feature in various guises, particularly as shoemakers discovered new ways of perfecting and strengthening the structure. Designs became more adventurous, particularly in shoes for women, and culminated in the extremely narrow-waisted heel design that simply became known as the French heel, and which reached new heights of up to 10 cm (4 in)

Critical courtier the Marquis of Marigny wrote a letter to Cardinal Montalto commenting that, 'I wear pointed shoes with a pad under the heel making me high enough to aspire to the title Royal Highness!' So important was the height of one's heels during this time, in fact, that wooden heels became the specialized work of a 'talonnier' (a heelpiece maker).

The French style also included a preference for large bows like windmill sails and, from the mid-seventeeth century, buckles. The latter offered a new method of fastening latchet shoes. Buckles were functional, but could also be highly decorative and appealed to the nobility throughout Europe, whose outward flamboyance read as an indication of wealth and status.

THE START OF AN AMERICAN SHOE INDUSTRY

At this time America was undergoing colony building and various conflicts with the indigenous Indian population. In 1685 James II consolidated New England Colonies, which subsequently took control of New England in 1686. The Hudson Bay Co. was formed in Canada in 1670.

In 1660 the General Assembly had brought in laws to control Virginia's up-and-coming shoe trade. All existing operations in Virginia's seventeen counties were ordered to operate at county expense as 'one or more tanhouses, and… provide tanners, curryers and shoemakers, to tanne, curry, and make the hides of the country into leather and shoes'. Al Saguto notes that between 1653 and 1658, licences in England were granted to export more than 45,600 pairs of shoes to Virginia, setting up a competitive economic environment between locally produced and imported goods.

THE RED HEEL

From the 1660s, the flamboyant King Louis XIV of France became the most influential man in Europe. Incredibly successful in creating a French court and surrounding himself with sycophantic noblemen, he contributed to the widespread influence of French society across the Continent and beyond.

Louis XIV was personally responsible for several trends during this period, including the wearing of luxuriant wigs and the adoption of the red heel and sole. Both read as indicators of his status, but they also compensated for his low stature for, measuring 1 m 65 cm (5 ft 5 in), the Sun King was a short man. High heels were fashionable at the time and, paired with towering wigs, they created an illusion of extra height. Such a significant part of the look, Louis's heels were covered in red Morocco leather or painted that colour. At times the King also wore heels painted with landscapes, battle scenes and – it has been suggested, risqué portraits – a number of which were the creations of the French royal shoemaker Nicholas Lestage.

THE ULTIMATE STATUS SYMBOL

The red was a symbol of wealth and, in Louis's case, his divine right as king. The effect was not only to raise the wearer above the masses, but to alert onlookers to a person's high status. First worn by Louis XIV, the style gradually filtered down – first through the French royal court, then on to the various social classes, and eventually carried across to England, where red heels featured on the shoes of both men and women.

Red heels became symbols of worldliness and sophistication. The style is echoed in the red soles of Christian Louboutin's shoes today (see pp. 248–9).

LEFT: *Portrait of King Louis XIV of France* by Hyacinthe Rigaud, 1701, Musée du Louvre, Paris. The French King wore shoes with red heels from his early twenties until he was at least sixty-three years old.

Louis XIV also contributed his name to the construction we refer to today as the Louis heel. At the time this was a solid wooden heel with a straight back line and an outward flare to the base. In modern versions of the design the back line has a concave curve. A high version of this heel is known as the 'Pompadour' (see p. 70).

RED IS THE COLOUR

Red has always been a significant and powerful colour, in part owing to the expense involved in obtaining red dye. The colour has been used to convey contrasting messages at different times and in different cultures. For example, wearing red shoes was a prerogative of Roman senators and, later, the emperor. Popes have worn red since the thirteenth century. Contemporary examples include Dorothy's ruby slippers in *The Wizard of Oz* and the demonic red ballet shoes that lead Vicky, the main character in the British film *The Red Shoes*, to her death.

Natural carmine dye is derived from cochineal scale insects. Originating in South America, it was in use from the fifteenth century. At one time, it was South America's second largest export after silver. Exported to Spain and used throughout Europe, it was used to dye the clothes of the very wealthy.

ABOVE: Women's green velvet mules embroidered in silver thread, 1670–89. The green velvet uppers are lined with pink satin over white kid and have blunt-pointed toes. They are embroidered in silver with broad bands across the instep; the design shows an Indian influence. The shoes have Louis heels that are 7.5 cm (3 in) high, covered in red Morocco leather.

EARLY BUCKLES

The most significant fashion event from 1660 onwards was the introduction of the highly decorative buckle. Small, plain and functional buckles had featured on shoes before this time, but models now completely transcended their practical use. Worn by men on plain, black leather latchet shoes, buckles of gold, silver, copper and brass (depending on social standing, naturally) became all the rage.

A portrait of English King Charles II by J M Wright (1661), now in Her Majesty the Queen's Collection, depicts the monarch in his coronation robes. He wears white leather shoes popular for ceremonial and court wear. They have French-style red heels and soles (see pp. 60–1) and a buckle attached to the latchets over a high tongue. The King was at the forefront of fashion, and it took a little longer for the wearing of buckles to filter down through the classes.

   Women were particularly late in adopting them, perhaps because they were not readily visible beneath long skirts and had a tendency to catch at the hem. However, although women favoured ribbon ties initially, the buckle did become the prevailing style until the French Revolution (1789).

LATCHET STYLE

It appears that, in most cases, the buckle was attached to the latchets and not to the upper of a shoe. Early versions of this new style involved a buckle with a stud that locked into a hole in one of the latchets. The second latchet was cut longer to fasten the shoe. Eventually latchets extended so that they overlapped across the instep and became wider to accommodate the buckle. A shift in shoe design in the first quarter of the eighteenth century saw more robust, heavier styles of shoe with larger buckles. Such shoes had wide latchets, each with a set of double prongs – the first to attach the buckle, the second to act as the fastener.

BUCKLE DESIGN

Initially, buckles were small and utilitarian – ovals or oblongs made from metal – sometimes set with stones of glass paste. But then, gradually, they got bigger and bigger. Most were cast and chased with decorative elements. Cut-glass and paste buckles worn by women became must-have accessories that a lady simply transferred from one favourite pair of shoes to another. For this reason, very few pairs of shoes have survived with their original buckles.

ABOVE: Women's buckles. Silver with gold bezel and cut glass, 1780s. They measure 7.5 cm (3 in) in width.

LEFT: Women's cut-glass and silver buckles dating from the eighteenth century. When they catch the light, these buckles really do sparkle.

RIBBON BOWS

Another fashion that appeared at around the same time was that of wide ribbon bows, seen on shoes worn by Louis XIV and his court in portraits. In 1660 Louis was presented with a pair of buckle latchet shoes sporting high, red heels and bows that were 40 cm (16 in) wide.

Generally, buckles and large ribbon laces were attached or fastened high on the instep over an extended tongue. In some cases these tongues on men's shoes were so long that they could be folded back to flop over the shoe. Taking advantage of the opportunity to add even more colour and decoration, the undersides of these tongues were stiffened and lined with coloured silks or cut into decorative shapes.

BELOW: Women's green satin buckle latchet shoes, *c.* 1750. They have a pointed up-curved toe and a 6 cm (2½ in) covered Louis heel.

WOMEN'S HEELS

Up until this time, styles of women's shoes had not differed significantly from those of men, yet from the 1660s a division was beginning to grow. Men spent more time out of doors and wore practical footwear that was suitable both for inside and out. Women, on the other hand, spent more time in the home.

In many respects women's shoes remained fairly constant in style during this period, with thick, reasonably high heels and pointed or prow-shaped toes. A popular style from the 1660s to the 1680s was characterized by a long, square toe, closed sides and a latchet-tie fastening. Such shoes also had high heels in carved wood that were covered with leather or a textile of some kind. Variations on the theme included shoes with blunter toes and lower heels, while a more feminine, pointed toe developed from the 1670s onwards.

A particular feature of women's shoes at this time was a white kid leather rand (the thin strip inserted between the sole and the upper). A fashionable detail, the rand also aided construction, as the shoemaker found it easier to stitch an often delicate textile upper to a softer rand than directly to the sole of the shoe.

On the whole, French styles were considerably more elegant than other European styles, and English equivalents looked rather clumsy by comparison.

DECORATIVE FEATURES

Women outstripped men when it came to decoration and embellishment. All manner of silks, brocades, appliqué braids and velvets became popular from the 1660s onwards. In England, the decorative use of bullion lace, made of woven gold and silver threads, was very fashionable and is thought to have been influenced by Catherine of Braganza, King Charles II's Portuguese queen. Shoemakers used the lace on the tongue and vamp of a shoe, and to cover the back seams. The style became so fashionable in England that Portuguese authorities were forced to ban its export across the Continent in 1711, for fear that their stocks would run out completely.

Common to fashions throughout Europe was the fact that shoes rarely matched a dress. In many cases, this was too complicated and too costly to achieve. A fashion for wearing long skirts obscured shoes anyway, particularly from a distance. Similar colours and patterned textiles may have been a feature on a lady's clothing, but it was not unusual to see completely contrasting outfits, too.

LEFT: An English man and two women of the mid-seventeenth century, engraved by James Peller Malcolm from an old source in his *Anecdotes of the Manners and Customs of London*.

OPPOSITE: Women's blue velvet, latchet-tie shoes with narrow, squared toes, c. 1660. The uppers have been embroidered with padded floral motifs in silver gilt thread, and the top edge bound in blue silk. The shoes are lined with white kid leather, have a white kid rand and a high, leather-covered Louis heel.

LACKING IN COMFORT

Women of this period must have found their shoes quite difficult to walk in for any length of time. It was not uncommon for heels to be placed too far forwards under the instep or for them to slope at a sharp angle, both of which tended to make a woman fall backwards. On the other hand, shoes with high heels forced a woman onto the balls of her feet, and this caused discomfort. There were also fears that the sole waist of a shoe might snap under the weight of its wearer. If worn outside, the thin soles and shallow styles of many shoes gave very little protection against stony or rough terrain.

Women were expected to walk in such shoes at assemblies, balls and visits to spas or places of interest, primarily so that they could show off their fashion sense and wealth. In reality, however, the sheer construction of the shoes made them better suited to indoor wear, where a lady could be within easy reach of a chair for relief.

THE DOMED TOE

A buckled latchet shoe in black was the norm for men at the end of the seventeenth century. The type of buckle worn gave an indication of the wearer's wealth and status as well as the importance of the occasion. Precious metals and stones reserved for the upper classes were replaced with steel, brass and pinchbeck for the less wealthy.

It might have been plain, but this style of shoe did much to emphasize the ankle, especially when combined with a pale coloured stocking. And at the time, an elegant ankle on a man was much admired. Shoes in lighter leathers became the reserve of court or ceremonial occasions, where buckles worn on breeches matched those on the shoes.

In the early years of the seventeenth century, wide-domed and square-toed shoes became popular. The style is reflected in a portrait of English King George I in his coronation robes, c. 1714. To balance the dominant toe shape, heels on such shoes were high and flared. This style was later replaced with the dull-pointed toe.

THE RETURN OF THE BOOT

In England, boots had become less fashionable following the Civil War – owing to their association with the armed conflict – only to return in the 1690s as fashionable footwear. The jackboot gradually replaced the cavalier's soft, wrinkled leather boots (see pp. 54–5). Possibly originating in Holland, the jackboot was made of much thicker and stiffer leather. It became a more solid boot, often with a high-wax finish. Jackboots could be thigh-high to protect the wearer from inclement weather and injury when fighting. Examples from the early 1700s sport the classic square-domed toe shape.

MEN'S MULES

Men's shoes became more practical for outdoor wear during this period, and while it was acceptable to sport shoes indoors, boots were deemed inappropriate house wear. Instead, men often wore what we would now call mules – backless shoes – in a variety of colours and materials, often elaborately embellished.

BELOW: Man's dark maroon, leather, slip-on shoe, 1714–20s, possibly French made. This example has an amazingly wide, square-domed toe and high, hollow heel flaring to a leather top piece pegged on. The tongue has traces of pink silk lining which, when turned over the instep, formed a cupid's bow. Men's shoes without buckle straps were rare at this time.

TOWARDS THE AGE OF REASON

BELOW: Men's silk brocade mule slippers, *c.* 1710, possibly French made. These show the wide, square-domed toe in a delightful pink, beige and green bizarre silk (figured silk fabric). Originally, the shoes would have had a strip of silver braid at the vamp top. They have a high, covered, flared heel and are straights. They would have been for indoor wear.

67

JOCKEYS, FOOTMEN AND GROOMS
THE JOCKEY BOOT

With the boot finding new favour from the 1690s onwards, a number of styles emerged for different activities, with riding, hunting, travel and military pursuits among them. In England, a craze for horse racing saw the emergence of a light jockey boot, first seen in the 1720s. Ending just below the knee, the boot had a higher, softer leather top that turned down to form a distinctive brown or pale leather cuff, pulled on by leather loops.

The style was popular with young men of the day, who were quite often labelled jockeys, footmen or grooms when seen in public. *The Universal Spectator* pointed to 'sparks who choose to appear as jockeys, seldom to be seen without boot' (1739), and a comment in *The Whole Art of Dress* remarked: 'I do not know how it is…we are apt in London to connect something very low with their appearance'.

The jockey boot is possibly the nearest the English have ever come to a national dress. Though not as popular abroad, the style was worn by men in France and America. While these foreign interpretations were slightly different from English versions, say in the shape of the toe, they would nevertheless have been called jockey boots.

By the 1780s this style was renamed the top boot and was very close fitting. A style with longevity, the jockey boot remains available today as an expensive riding boot and periodically appears in high-street fashion.

LEFT: Men's black, Bordeaux calf leather, racing jockey boot, 1911, possibly made by Palmer Brothers, Newmarket. This boot weighs 255 g (9 oz) and was hand-sewn.

BELOW: A close race at Newmarket, between Gray Windham and Bay Bottom, c. 1710. The jockeys are wearing the boot that inspired so many wearers in the 1720s. Original artwork after John Wootton.

RIGHT: Thick and heavy leather postilion boots, c. 1750s. Impressions around the leg tops were to receive straps for attaching to stirrups so that the rider could get in and out of them easily. Worn throughout Europe, this type of boot eventually became obsolete in the 1820s.

POSTILION BOOTS

Postilion boots were huge, protective riding boots made from thick leather. Hung on either side of a horse like baskets, the boots were worn by post boys and postilion riders. The boot was large enough to fit any foot and usually worn without a shoe, although later on, light leather slip-on shoes were worn, too. Postilions rode the leading horse of a team or pair drawing a coach or carriage. This was an important job, particularly in the absence of a coachman. The boots protected the rider from bad weather and possible injury as he raced to reach his destination on time. Postilion boots were common in Britain from the mid-seventeenth century to around 1830, when better roads made them redundant. In parts of Europe they continued for longer.

THE FRENCH HEEL

With French styles dominating during this period, Paris was a great source of fashion inspiration. Although the rest of Europe avoided slavishly emulating the excesses of French fashions, various countries adopted the main styles to a certain degree. Among the more widespread of these was the high 'French' or 'Pompadour' heel, most often seen on a mule.

Named after Madame de Pompadour, mistress to King Louis XV, the heel was incredibly narrow-waisted and curved inwards beneath the instep. They were notoriously difficult to walk in, but made the most fantastic boudoir shoe.

As is so often the case, small was considered beautiful when it came to wearing the French heel. There are tales of women binding their feet to make them look smaller and also of ladies fainting owing to the constriction and discomfort caused. Such heels invariably caused a degree of contemporary satirical comment (see quote).

Of course, such shoes were only for the very wealthy and there were many heel variations – from high and slender, to thick and chunky. In terms of decoration, brocaded silks and wool remained very popular, but examples of painted leather shoes and those made from woven straw also existed. Mules in general – with or without the Pompadour heel – were popular for indoor and outdoor wear (at least at balls). These mules were known as slippers.

OPPOSITE: *The Swing* by Jean-Honoré Fragonard, *c.* 1767. A young lady kicks off her beautifully heeled shoe as an elderly man pushes her into the air on a swing. The gesture is made towards a lover hiding in the bushes below.

'Mount on French heels, When you go to the ball –

'Tis the fashion to totter and show you can fall.'

(Lines from an eighteenth-century satirical poem)

RIGHT: Women's rust-coloured, silk damask mules, 1720–50. They have silver braid down the centre of the vamp and come to a distinct point over the instep. They have a 10 cm (4 in) covered heel and are possibly French made, for salon wear.

PATTEN EVOLUTION

During the eighteenth and nineteenth centuries, the practical solution for raising oneself out of the mud and the wet was the iron-ringed patten. At its simplest, this involved a rough, foot-shaped piece of wood, the toe of which echoed the shape in fashion at the time. Worn beneath a person's shoes, a patten had leather latchet ties that came up over the foot for tying securely. Some variations also had leather toecaps.

An iron stalk was attached to the patten, at the end of which was an iron ring, usually oval in shape. The idea was that as the iron ring made contact with the ground, it distributed the wearer's weight and aided mobility.

These pattens must have been very difficult to walk in, since there was no flexibility in the solid wooden platform. A certain amount of leg lifting and stomping action was necessary, unless one could master the glide, which was difficult on uneven surfaces. As with pattens of the Middle Ages (see pp. 36–7), hinges were added to some styles in an attempt to increase flexibility.

A LOWER-CLASS PHENOMENON

Highly functional and cumbersome in appearance, pattens did not appeal to the aristocracy and were generally worn by the less wealthy and countryside dwellers. In 1725 Daniel Defoe published *Every-Body's Business is No-Body's Business*, a pamphlet on the breakdown of the social order. In it, he highlighted the problem of a country girl aspiring to look like her mistress by swapping her 'high wooden pattens' for 'leather clogs' when she came to work in London.

'Patynmakers' are first mentioned in City of London records in 1379 and a pair of pattens features in the *Arnolfini Portrait* of 1434 (see p. 36). They were worn across Northern Europe, Italy and other countries to raise the wearer out of the mud on the streets.

CLOG OVERSHOES

If pattens were for country folk and the working classes, then clog overshoes were for the upper classes. These small, odd-looking overshoes consisted of textile uppers and leather soles, with the most practical versions being made entirely of leather. The clog's sole fitted beneath the wearer's shoe and was curved and shaped in such a way that it fitted snugly within the arch of the shoe, leaving an area to accommodate the heel at the back. The style was not as practical for outdoors, however, and quickly became little more than a fashion accessory. Wealthy patrons ordered a pair of shoes from their shoemaker, who at the same time could make a pair of matching overshoes for showing off when companions came to visit.

THE PADUKA

The paduka is India's oldest footwear. The open design is suited to the climate, as the shoes keep the sole raised above the sun-baked ground.

Within the Hindu religion, cows are considered holy animals and therefore footwear made of cow leather is not desirable. Shoes worn by holy people – or in holy spaces – were therefore made of wood, ivory, metal and, sometimes, camel leather. Holy men wore simple wooden padukas, while examples worn by well-off worshippers tended to be more elaborate.

The Hindu deities Krishna and Rama are often depicted wearing padukas. The shoes can be easily removed before entering a sacred space, such as a temple. This paduka is plain, with intricate carving and a very shapely footbed.

RIGHT: Single silk and leather clog overshoe c. 1700. You can see clearly where the heel would be accommodated.

BELOW: Women's buckle latchet shoes with matching clog overshoes in a floral silk brocade/damask, 1680–1720. The shoes have 5 cm (2 in) heels covered in red, Morocco leather. It is difficult to match up clogs with shoes but these have the same binding. The clog overshoes would have prevented wear to the shoe sole, but offered little practical protection from dirty, wet streets. They became must-have fashion accessories, indicating a rich and, therefore, more sedentary lifestyle.

5

RETURN TO SIMPLICITY

1750s TO THE 1840s

GROWING MARKETS

By the mid-eighteenth century, the Western world was rapidly moving towards an industrial age and the rate of change accelerated in tandem with the technical developments afoot. Europe's upper classes – and rising middle classes – began to invest in emerging industries, creating a market for luxury goods on an unprecedented scale. Customers with newfound wealth wanted to spend their money on the most conspicuous displays possible and this included buying the most fashionable ensembles of the day, with equally splendid pairs of shoes.

Increased prosperity, and the opportunity for more people to travel greater distances, meant that influences were coming from farther afield. This was the age of the Grand Tour, which saw many young European men travelling, in particular to Italy, in an effort to widen their cultural knowledge.
   In Great Britain, although the Industrial Revolution had little impact on the shoe industry itself, the development of better roads and a railway network from the 1830s onwards paved the way for easier and more comprehensive distribution of footwear across the country and farther afield. Queen Victoria's accession to the throne in 1837 heralded the start of the British Empire, which saw British-made footwear travel the world, and the importation of foreign-made footwear, too.

REVOLUTION AND WARFARE

French and Italian influences are evident in the high heels seen on women's footwear from the 1750s and 1760s. However, in response to political events, a greater taste for simplicity was developing, and fast. This came to a head by the French Revolution of 1789, the repercussions of which were felt throughout Europe. Big, brassy buckles reached their ostentatious peak in the 1770s, only to find rejection during the fashion watershed of the French Revolution. The heel met with criticism, too, and by the end of this period the majority of women's shoe styles were flat. In some cases women's shoes were so delicate that they were rarely suitable for wearing out of doors.

This period also saw an increase in demand for boots on two fronts. America called upon British bootmakers to contribute to supplies during their War of Independence (1775–83). On mainland Europe, the Napoleonic Wars (1799–1815) saw the arrival of new boot designs both for the battlefield and at home.

A NEW CONTENDER

Immediately following independence from Britain, Americans – flushed with their newfound sense of freedom – turned from British influences to those of France. Americans were also beginning to respond to home-grown fashions for the first time – a trend that looked set to continue from the mid-nineteenth century onwards. In 1830 *Godey's Lady's Book* was established. Initially the magazine had a remit for promoting women's education, but within a couple of decades it was publishing the first fashion plates.

Industry-wise, shoemaking in the United States increased in numbers and, in 1789, the Society of Master Cordwainers was established – largely, it seems, to protect the master shoemakers from competitors who were selling footwear too cheaply. Since there were no provisions for storing footwear, shoes had to be sold as quickly as possible, and this meant that selling could take place on the open market without the need for a stated price. The Federal Society of Journeymen Cordwainers was organized in 1794 and by 1835 the United Beneficial Society of Journeymen Cordwainers was established in Philadelphia. Shoemaking in America was a fast-growing profession and rapidly becoming much more organized.

GLOBAL INFLUENCES

Increased prosperity and opportunities for more people to travel greater distances meant that influences on shoe styles started to come from farther afield. Italian fashions came to the fore from the middle of the eighteenth century, with men adopting low-cut models with extravagant buckles. Conversely, the influence of Italian trends on women's footwear was not one of conspicuous foppish excess but, rather, a quiet reduction in heel height.

THE ITALIAN HEEL

The 'Italian' heel began to appear on shoes from the 1760s onwards. Incredibly slender, and much shorter than the French heel of the first half of the eighteenth century (see pp. 70–1), many designs involved the addition of a small wedge that enabled the shoe to support the wearer's weight. Now that the heel was so small and thin, this was a necessity. Carved from wood, the heel was typically covered in leather or textile, sometimes in a contrasting colour to the shoe – an effective fashion feature.

These were incredibly elegant shoes, much admired with the slightly shorter dress styles that made an appearance in the 1770s and 1780s. The rich brocaded silks and damasks of earlier styles began to give way to an altogether subtler palette of brocaded designs and plain satins.

Although easier to walk in, and despite the modifications discussed above, the slender heel was still prone to breaking. Some versions had a metal spike inserted into the centre of the heel, which made them quite dangerous. At least the

women wearing such footwear would have found it easier to navigate out of doors, since the first effective acts towards the provision of pavements took place at around this time.

THE PROW TOE

A stylized and fanciful Chinese influence was popular in Europe for short time in the 1780s. Chinoiserie captured the imagination of those decorating the interiors of large houses with the latest fashions. For a short few years around 1786, 'Chinese' looking shoes became popular. These slip-on shoes were made of leather – often in black, green or red. Conforming to the heel styles of the day – low, slim and small wedges – the most distinctive feature of these shoes was an upturned prow toe.

BELOW: Woman's red leather shoe in the Chinese taste, c. 1786. The shoe has a pointed, upturned (prow) toe and wedged Italian heel covered in black leather.

LEFT: Women's black and white (originally yellow) kid shoes with an Italian heel, c. 1795. These shoes belonged to Miss Percival, the sister of the Rt Hon Spencer Percival, MP for Northampton, 1797–1812. He became prime minister on 4 October 1809 and has the distinction of being the only PM to be assassinated. He was shot by John Bellingham, a merchant with a grievance against the government, who shot him dead in the lobby of the House of Commons.

BELOW: Women's green leather shoes in the Chinese taste, c. 1786. They have a narrow, upturned, pointed toe.

SHOE SUPERSTITIONS
FOLLOWING TRADITION

Shoes are ancient and should be considered in many more ways than just the practical. They express a person's identity and cultural background and indicate social status, class, gender, trade and religion.

Shoes can also signify a power quite independent of any wearer and can play an important part in people's lives. Think how many sayings involve shoes – to put the boot in, if the shoe fits, living on a shoestring and down at heel are just a few of them. The number of shoe superstitions is an indication of just how powerful and mysterious they are.

- A girl can find out who she'll marry on Midsummer Eve if she places her shoes by the bed and chants:
  Point your shoes toward the street,
  Leave your garters on your feet;
  Put your stocking on your head,
  And you'll dream of the man you're going to wed.

- Probably the most common shoe superstition is that shoes must never be placed on a table. Many people believe this only applies to new shoes, and often the penalty varies. Some versions forecast ill luck or a quarrel, whilst others promise 'you'll never marry' or even imminent death!

- Shoes are traditionally associated with going on a journey. From at least the sixteenth century onwards, a way of wishing somebody good luck on a journey was to throw an old shoe after them. In 1855 Queen Victoria wrote in her journal of her arrival at Balmoral: 'an old shoe was thrown after us into the house, for good luck'.

- Shoes are linked to fertility and often appear at weddings. The old boot tied to the back of the bride and groom's car is a survivor of the custom of throwing a shoe over the bride and groom to ensure that the marriage was successful in terms of children.

- In the nineteenth century, wives and friends of sailors threw shoes at the whaling ships as they passed Whitby Pier head en route to Greenland, to hope for a safe ocean journey.

- In Morocco if a man finds a slipper in the road he'll soon find a wife.

- In China a childless woman wishing for a child carried beautifully embroidered doll-size shoes and placed them in shrines.

- In Germany it is believed that a wife who wears her husband's slippers on their wedding day will have an easy labour.

- In China boys would often wear shoes with tiger faces on them to ward off evil spirits and keep the wearer safe.

- It is believed that you should always put the right shoe on first, and if you don't bad luck will follow. This probably originates in Roman times. If you accidentally put the wrong shoe on first, you must take it off, go outside and have someone throw the shoe after you.

- In Ireland it is tempting fate to wear a new pair of shoes at a funeral. A person who does is warned he'll not live to wear them out or next time he wears them it will be at his own funeral!

- In India a magician would beat hailstones with a shoe to stop a storm.

- In India a wife could make her husband obedient by feeding him a loaf made with flour weighing the same as her left shoe.

- According to some legends, the best way to forget all your troubles is to wear tight shoes!

- Some say that new shoes squeak when they have not been paid for!

- In ancient Egypt the cure for a headache was to inhale the smoke from burning sandals.

ABOVE: Shoes have always been related to fertility as the following nursery rhyme implies: 'There was an old lady who lived in a shoe; She had so many children, she didn't know what to do; She gave them some broth without any bread; Then whipped them all soundly and put them to bed.'

BELOW: Covered with confetti, this shoe was made by the female employees of Sears Factory and given as a wedding gift to a colleague in 1923. In the United Kingdom it is the custom to throw or tie shoes to the back of the newlyweds' car. Loaded with symbolism, the shoes may be wishing the newlyweds good luck, hoping for a large family or symbolizing the passing of the bride from her father to the groom.

THE ARTOIS BUCKLE

By the 1770s, buckles for both men and women had reached their largest and most spectacular manifestation, culminating in the Artois style in 1777, named after the French Comte d'Artois, later to become Charles X. Men wore their buckles on plain black latchet shoes with low-stacked heels. Elegant in the extreme, these shoes provided the perfect canvas for displaying wonderfully over-the-top Artois buckles.

During the 1770s, these large shoe buckles caught the attention of a particular group of fashionable young men. Known as 'macaronis', they wore very high wigs, tightly cut coats and breeches in pastel shades, and – according to their critics – too much perfume. The term 'macaroni' applied to young European men who had the privilege and wealth to undertake the Grand Tour. Such men had been exposed to all things stylish and elegant, particularly in Italy, and many young fops adopted this new style of dressing.

AN EFFEMINATE STYLE

Side seams on footwear gradually moved down towards the toe, which enabled macaronis to wear buckles very low down the shoe (causing all manner of problems in keeping the shoes on and in place). The buckles were so large and weighty – up to 220–250 g (8–10 oz) in some cases – that they pulled the front of the shoe down, while the back rose up in protest. In 1782 the German author Karl Philipp Moritz was greatly irritated by a young fop who was sitting behind him at a London theatre, who 'continually put his foot on my bench in order to show off the flashy stone buckles on his shoes; if I didn't make way for his precious buckles he put his foot on my coat tails.'

In addition to buckles made from various precious and non-precious metals, new materials were tested such as Wedgwood jasper cameos, bone and ceramic pearlware. In much of Europe, as wealth increased down the social scale, even the lower classes could satisfy their desire for large buckles made from cheaper materials, available owing to advances in manufacturing techniques.

LEFT: This wonderful engraving, *c.* 1773, shows a rather shallow-looking and irritating young 'macaroni' smirking and suppressing a giggle.

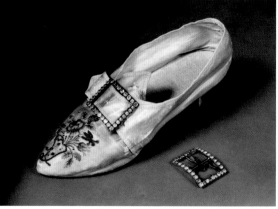

LEFT: One of a pair of ivory silk, buckle latchet shoes embroidered on the vamps, 1784. The buckles are silver, set with paste.

BELOW: A pair of silver buckles set with pastes and green and white enamel, *c.* 1785. They are housed in a delightful and original, purpose-made, shaped, gold-tooled, red Morocco leather case.

'All our young fops of quality, and even the lowest of our people in London, wear coach-harness buckles, the latter in brass, white metal and pinchbeck.'

The Gentlemen's Magazine, June 1777.

CHANGING FASHIONS

Throughout Europe, women's fashions were largely dictated by reactions to the French Revolution and the radical social and political turmoil of 1789. The French ideals of 'Liberté, égalité, fraternité' did not sit well with the conspicuous displays of wealth that large, over-the-top shoe buckles provided. 'Down with buckles' was the cry of the Parisian masses in 1789.

As shoe expert June Swann states: 'The buckle was killed by the desire for equality'. Shoe buckle manufacturers throughout Europe were hit hard. Buckles didn't simply disappear overnight, however. As with many trends, the process was gradual, radiating out from fashionable centres, but they did eventually disappear.

PREVAILING STYLES

The French Revolution, and the downfall of the monarchy in particular, did much to damage France's reputation – and Paris, once the epicentre of all things tasteful, went silent.

This silence was short-lived, however, and as the eighteenth century drew to a close, French fashions were once again a major influence across Europe.

Women's shoes developed throughout Europe in tandem with the prevailing French styles. Broad, flat heels emerged, and there was a brief passion for the 'sandle' shoe – a low-cut, slip-on model fastened with ribbons that tied around the ankle and lower leg. Shoe styles tended towards the simple, providing greater freedom of movement. They reflected the narrow look of French fashions, with a distinct pointed toe and a low Italian heel, with or without a wedge. Colours were minimal, often with shoes in a single tone throughout. Cream, white and black were very popular although colours such as yellow, olive and blue also existed, designed to match a wearer's other accessories and clothing.

Shoes were often accompanied by small leather overshoes, which covered the toe and had an elasticated loop that went around the heel. Slip-on shoes, rather like a court shoe, were common in black, often with a cut-out design on the vamp that had a coloured leather insert – delicately reminiscent of the cuts and slashes seen on medieval footwear in the past (see pp. 32–3).

BOTTOM LEFT: Women's heliotrope (purplish-red, but faded to steel blue) satin over kid leather shoes, c. 1796. They have pointed toes and 4 cm (1½ in) wedge-shaped heels covered in white kid leather. The edges are bound with blue braid and there are drawstrings around the vamps. The shoes are embroidered with silver thread and sequins, both now tarnished.

BELOW: Women's rose pink, kid leather, slip-on shoes, 1810–19. The uppers are decorated with a white scalloped design. They have silk ribbon loops and ties to go around the ankle and low, covered, wedge heels. They are an example of a sandle shoe.

SHOELACES AND SIDE TIES

From the 1790s, shoes were characterized by a long toe, which garnered a certain amount of critical comment. The buckled latchet-style shoe gradually gave way to a new trend (for the upper classes, at least) for lace-up shoes and shoe ribbons. Similar developments were seen in the latest boot styles.

Owing to their association with the working classes, shoestrings had fallen out of favour during the first half of the eighteenth century, but attitudes were beginning to change. Looking for simpler, more comfortable styles, men and women rejected the flamboyant buckles of the 1770s (see pp. 82–3). In practical terms, it was much easier to keep the low-cut styles of the preceding decades on one's feet using laces. According to *The Whole Art of Dress*, 'The tie should be of broad ribbon, made into a small double bow'. Coloured leather was a popular choice for such shoes, particularly in red or white. The use of patent leather also gained favour across Europe and in America.

THE HALF-BOOT

By the beginning of the nineteenth century, boots had made a reappearance to the extent that boot-closer-turned-author James Devlin, in his guide to the trade, *The Shoemaker*, wrote: 'At present we are emphatically a booted people, so are the French and the Americans'. By this time it had become acceptable for middle- and upper-class women to wear boots. Half-boots with front lacing and trimmed decoration were available, as were side-lacing boots, fastened with lace and a brass or wire tag. Knotted through the bottom hole, the lace threaded over and up through the holes to the top of the boot.

The arbiter of men's fashion at the English court, George 'Beau' Brummell, set the bar for men's appearance by promoting restraint, neatness, cleanliness and simplicity in all aspects of dress. At the same time, Brummell made a feminine take on fashion more acceptable, although tales that he had his boots cleaned and polished with champagne do little for his supposedly inclusive reputation!

OPPOSITE: Men's red, leather, lace-up shoes, c. 1790. They have very long quarters and a 1 cm (½ in) covered heel. Given their lovely colour, they may have been for holiday wear, possibly by the seaside.

BELOW: Women's wool, side-lace boots in stripes of brown, fawn and blue, with black patent toes and heels, 1850–9. The boots have narrow, square toes and flat soles. The black lace has a little brass tag.

RIGHTS AND LEFTS

It was during the 1790s that right and left shoes were reintroduced. Most shoe styles during this period were flat-soled, and it became much easier for a shoemaker to make a mirror-image last.

This, coupled with the invention of the pantograph (an instrument for copying a drawing on a different scale using a system of hinged and jointed rods), meant that

rights and lefts eventually replaced straights.

The renowned American bootmaker, William Young of Philadelphia, is credited with the invention of rights and lefts but, as with many boot and shoe innovations, it is difficult to attribute such an invention to any one person. In general, men adopted the return of rights and lefts quicker than women.

TOOLS OF THE TRADE
SHOEMAKING APPRENTICESHIPS

The concept of teaching the young a trade by binding them to a master for instruction is one that dates back to ancient times. Shoemakers are known to have offered apprenticeships in England, and doubtless farther afield, from the Middle Ages onwards. Such practices have long been prone to exploitation and, by this time, most trades were subject to guild rules when dealing with apprentices.

THE ENGLISH MODEL

England's largest shoemaking region at the time was around the town of Northampton, and this serves as a good example of how the system worked in general. Children began working at five to six years old and were apprenticed from the age of seven onwards, usually for a minimum of seven years. By the fourteenth century, this had become the recognized route to citizenship and therefore emancipation. Guilds supervised each child, with stiff premiums payable at commencement, and low wages to cover the cost of learning and the privileges that would ensue at the end.

Northampton's Guild was formed in 1401. Each master was restricted to a maximum of three apprentices (other towns might limit it to one) who were usually apprenticed between the ages of seven to eleven. For those boys who 'lived in', the master provided food, lodging and clothing. At the end of his term the master gave a boy a double set of apparel – including shoes – and a set of tools for the trade, though the double apparel set stopped about 1660.

HOW THE SYSTEM PROGRESSED

In 1593 the Statute of Artificers regulated apprenticeship on a national, instead of guild, basis. Each was to serve for seven years, could not be bound until the age of twelve and was to work for twelve hours a day in summer and all the daylight hours in winter. This was not repealed until 1814.

By the time of the Civil War, a master stopped providing everything for an apprentice and it was down to the parents to provide most of his apparel. By the 1600s, parents were expected to provide lodgings, food, drink and, in some cases, an apron and tools. Where specified, the wages in the seventeenth century were nothing in the first year, six shillings a week in the second year, then rose in sixpences to two shillings and sixpence in the sixth and seventh years.

As the shoemaking trade increased, and with warehouses in London selling country-made shoes, the number of apprentices increased, though many learned their trade

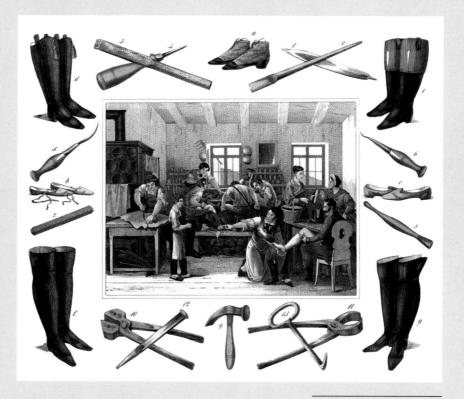

by working as journeymen rather than being formally apprenticed. With the increase in trade came an opportunity for exploitation and mistreatment. Some shoemakers stipulated high premiums, which rose in the later 1770s following demands for extra footwear during the American War of Independence.

By 1785 wages increased to eighteen shillings in the first year and then by sixpence increments. By 1800 the large quantities of footwear required during the Napoleonic Wars and the insatiable demand of the growing cities both in Britain and Europe for British-made footwear meant that the apprenticeship system was overwhelmed, with only a small percentage of men now being apprenticed in shoemaking towns. By the mid-nineteenth century, apprenticeships in the large shoemaking towns had ceased. They may have been taken on by shoemakers in small towns and villages, but it was a dying system.

Although demand for footwear was steadily increasing as the population rose and expanding foreign markets grew, the end of the 1850s saw the rise of the first proper factories; the old apprenticeship system was no longer valid.

ABOVE: *Profession: Shoemaker*, a lithograph from Eßlingen, Germany, *c.* 1860. It belongs to a series of lithographs showing the workplaces of thirty handcraftsmen (*Dreißig Werkstätten von Handwerkern*).

LEFT: Men's black patent and green leather dress wellington boots, 1840-49. This pair illustrates beautifully the skill and craftsmanship of the shoemaker, who has spent many years learning his trade.

HOME-MADE SHOES

So simple were the designs of women's footwear at the turn of the nineteenth century that European and American ladies who tired of tapestry, reading or playing the piano for amusement were able to turn their hands to shoemaking. In order to satisfy this new-found recreation, shoe patterns began to appear in women's journals of the day.

In England in 1808, the Honourable Mrs Calvert wrote: 'I began a new science today – shoemaking. It is all the fashion. I had a master with me for two hours, and I think I shall be able to make very nice shoes. It amuses me and occupies me, which at present is very useful to me.' From *An Irish Beauty of the Regency* compiled from *Mes Souvenirs*, the unpublished journals of the Hon. Mrs Calvert 1798–1822, by Mrs Warrenne Black, 1911.

In the *Boot and Shoe Maker* magazine, there is a small snippet that reads: 'Young man, if you should see your girl gazing intently at your feet, don't shift them about uneasily, or draw them up to sit upon them, under the impression she is overwhelmed by their immense size. She is merely taking their measure, mentally for a pair of slippers, on the toes of which she intends to work a blue dog, with a green tail and scarlet ears' (25 October 1879).

Sadly, without any written provenance, it is difficult to distinguish home-made shoes from this period since all women's shoes would have been made by hand at this time.

AN ESTABLISHED TRADITION

In fact, women had an even earlier presence in the making of shoes. Wives of shoemakers frequently helped their husbands 'close' the upper. The process involved sewing the upper components of the shoe together and was particularly suited to women at a time when shoe uppers were made mostly from textiles (from the seventeenth century onwards). Once the first factories were established in the 1860s, similar divisions of labour existed, generally with women employed in the closing room – only now they stitched the uppers using sewing machines.

In the illustration from an article titled 'The Northampton Shoemaker' in *Good Words* magazine, 1 November 1869, women are shown employed in a machine-closer's premises in the town (see top right). Each would have worked from 7.00 a.m. until 6.00 p.m. with an hour's break for lunch.

ABOVE: In this illustration of a closing room, 1869, the young women seated on the left sew (close) the uppers using treadle sewing machines; children in the middle tie knots at the ends of the machinists' threads; and the young women on the right are fitters, whose job it is to fit together the sections of the uppers before passing them to the machinists. One woman appears to be hammering the seams flat.

LEFT: Women's black, satin, slip-on shoes, 1830–9. As you can see from the soles, they are not straights, but are made with a distinct right and left shoe. Their white kid leather quarter lining is inscribed: Miss Marshall Right.

RIGHT AND BELOW: Two from a set of four pairs of women's slip-on shoes all made by Melnotte of Paris, c. 1830. They are in a specially made linen bag that is fastened with buttons and has compartment pockets for each pair.

MILITARY FOOTWEAR

The Napoleonic Wars of 1799–1815 sparked a widespread interest in all things military. The production of military dress rose steeply in order to satisfy the needs of the many men sent to fight. Inevitably, military clothing was seen in domestic circles too, and this included the prevailing styles of military footwear.

THE HESSIAN BOOT

Originally associated with light cavalry, the hessian boot became popular from 1795 until the 1830s. This very distinctive and expensive jet-black boot reached to just below the knee, and a tassel hung from a V-shaped dip at the centre front. This was a high-maintenance style and wearers often required the aid of a manservant to keep them highly polished and jet black. In *The Whole Art of Dress*, it states: 'In undress it is impossible to dress a fine leg, more especially of a short person, to a greater advantage than in a hessian'. In some cases the tassels on these boots reached exaggerated proportions and became a hindrance when worn beneath the trouser leg. The response was to cut the top of the boot straight and bind the edge. By doing this the tassel was lost.

Though worn for longer in America, the hessian boot was superseded in England by the wellington (see pp. 94–5), partly owing to reasons of sheer practicality.

THE BLUCHER BOOT

The Blucher boot was an open-tabbed, front-lace boot with a straight side seam. The style was named after Gebhard Leberecht von Blücher, general of the Prussian army, who fought on Wellington's side at the Battle of Waterloo (1815).

Originally the quarters involved a single piece of leather with no back seam. *The Whole Art of Dress* reported that: 'The boot is invented doubtless, for the mere purpose of saving trouble in dress, for without attending to silk stockings or the trouble of tying bows, you have merely to slip on the boots, and you are featly equipped in a moment'.

The British man became so associated with boots that the trend influenced men's fashion in Europe. Young French dandies took to wearing them, to the dismay of French commentators. General John Burgoyne mentions in 1780 that, 'Young fellows so fond of boots at all hours except when on horseback…then nothing but white trousers and a pair of dancing pumps.'

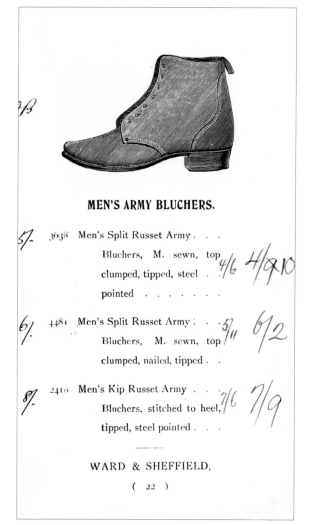

MEN'S ARMY BLUCHERS.

3638 Men's Split Russet Army . . . Bluchers, M. sewn, top clumped, tipped, steel pointed . . . .

4481 Men's Split Russet Army . . . Bluchers, M. sewn, top clumped, nailed, tipped . .

2416 Men's Kip Russet Army . . . Bluchers, stitched to heel, tipped, steel pointed . . .

WARD & SHEFFIELD,

(22)

LEFT: An advertisement for a military Blucher boot from a catalogue of Ward & Sheffield, Earls Barton, Northamptonshire, *c.* 1907.

ALTERNATE FEET

A return to rights and lefts, rather than straights (see p. 44), did cause some problems. In *The Art and Mystery of the Cordwainer*, author John F Rees reported that: 'If the wearer do not tread even, the shoe must wear much on one side' (1813). Soldiers habitually swapped their boots from right to left, as the standing order by the King's Shropshire Light Infantry in 1800 were told: 'Soldiers will wear their boots on alternate feet on alternate days'.

RIGHT: The Duke of Wellington sports a fine pair of hessians in this meeting with Admiral Nelson, *c.* 1890. This lithograph is held at the National Army Museum, London.

THE WELLINGTON BOOT

Today the word 'wellington' is used to describe a waterproof rubber boot worn for work or leisure. However it originally referred to a new shape of leather boot that was named after the military commander Arthur Wellesley. A celebrated hero, Wellesley became the first Duke of Wellington and won many victories against the French during the Napoleonic Wars – most famously the Battle of Waterloo in 1815.

Wellington was renowned for his interest in good quality footwear, and was often shown wearing hessian boots (see p. 93). In *The Soldiers' Feet and Footgear*, Captain Cecil Webb-Johnson notes: 'Wellington, when asked the most important part of a soldier's equipment, replied "Firstly, a pair of good shoes, secondly a second pair of good shoes, and thirdly a pair of half-soles"'(1913). For Wellington, Pry's cartoon (see right) – probably a very clever marketing ploy to capitalize on his victories – sealed the association.

George Hoby, bootmaker to St James's Palace, London, made Wellington's boots. Bata Shoe Museum is in possession of a letter from Wellington to Hoby that highlights how difficult it must have been to make them fit correctly. Two pairs of new boots ordered and received get the following response: 'The boots you sent me were still too small in the calf of the leg and about an inch and a half short of the leg.' So close-fitting was the wellington that one needed boot jacks to pull the boots off.

TAKING WELLINGTON'S NAME

Queen Victoria once asked the Duke of Wellington what type of boots he was wearing. 'People call them wellingtons, ma'am', he said. 'How absurd', commented the Queen, replying, 'Where, I should like to know, would they find a pair of wellingtons?' She obviously thought he was unique.

There is also a lovely story from the *St Crispin Journal*: 'One day, when Lord Brougham had driven to the house in the vehicle of his own invention, which Robinson the coach-maker had christened after him, he was met in the robing room by the Duke of Wellington, who after a low bow, accosted him: "I have always hitherto lived under the impression that your Lordship will go down to prosperity as the great apostle of education, the emancipator of the negro, the reformer of the law; but no – you will hereafter be known as the inventor of the carriage"…"And I my Lord Duke, have always been under the delusion that your grace would be remembered as the hero of a hundred battles, the

A WELLINGTON BOOT
Or the Head of the Army

LEFT: *A Wellington Boot or The Head of the Army*, by Paul Pry, 1827. This caricature of Wellington suggests that, in order to command successfully, one must have an intellectual head, but also the force of the boot – an important part of any soldier's war.

liberator of Europe, the conqueror of Napoleon; but no – your grace will be known as the inventor of pair of boots"…"damn the boots; I had forgotten them. You have the best of it"' (vol. II, 1869).

VARIATIONS IN STYLE

Dress wellingtons, or opera boots, have a black silk stocking over a tan leather lining and a silk top. The stocking is attached to a black patent galosh with a bow on the vamp top edge. Worn beneath trousers these had the appearance of a smart dress pump. Made in a myriad of colours, the legs were often fashioned from Morocco leather. James Devlin in *The Shoemaker* writes, 'some have green legs, some purple, some yellow, some made of black Spanish and some of white grain calf'. By the 1860s the wellington made way for a new style of ankle boot. However, it remained popular in the United States, where men wore them with the trouser leg tucked into the boot.

OPPOSITE: Men's red Morocco and black patent leather wellingtons, 1860–9.

A REJECTION OF EXCESS

From the turn of the nineteenth century, the heel on women's footwear became lower and lower, until it disappeared altogether. Toe shapes softened until, by the 1840s, the typical style for women was the simple, flat-soled, square-toed, slip-on shoe, with ribbon ties to help keep the shoes on the foot.

'Flats', as this style of shoes was known, complemented the fashions of the day for large puffed sleeves, tiny pulled-in waists and bell-shaped skirts. As skirts increased in fullness, so they became shorter in length. Naturally, all eyes were drawn to the foot, typically shod in jewel-coloured silk and satin slip-on shoes or ankle boots. Although colours such as yellow, purple, blue and red were common, there were many cream, white and black pairs available, too. Incredibly fragile, these little slippers – forerunners of the ballet shoe – were intended for indoor wear only. One evening's dancing at a ball would have created serious problems, as the following anecdotal story highlights.

Empress Josephine, the spouse of Napoleon Bonaparte, was said to have owned over three hundred pairs of these slippers. To her horror, she discovered one day that one shoe had a hole in its sole. She summoned her shoemaker and said, 'Look, this is dreadful, what are you going to do about it,' and the shoemaker is supposed to have replied: 'But ah madam I know what the problem is. You've worn them!' Whether a flight of shoe fancy or not, this tale highlights the fact that these slippers were not at all robust.

1812 *Costumes Parisiens* (1230)

Chapeau de Gros de Naples. Canezou et Robe de Perkale.

LEFT: *Costumes Parisiens,* c. 1812. The emerging fashion for shorter hemlines exposed a lady's ankles and, therefore, the prettiest shoes in the latest Parisian styles.

FIT FOR A BRIDE

Queen Victoria's wedding shoes sum up the simpler style perfectly. They are flat-soled with a satin upper, square toe and square throat, with ribbon ties. The Honiton ribbon appliqué on the vamp echoes the Honiton lace incorporated into her wedding dress. Queen Victoria was married on 10 February 1840.

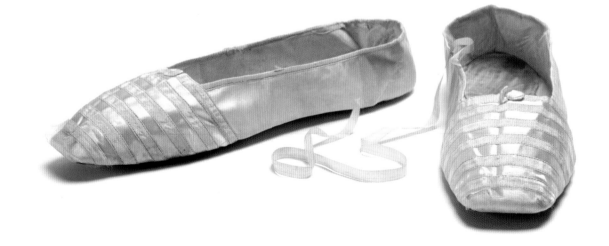

RIGHT AND BELOW LEFT: Queen Victoria's wedding shoes were made by Gundry & Sons Boot & Shoemakers to the Queen, the Queen Dowager, Their Royal Highnesses the Duchess of Kent & Princess Sophia, 1840. The firm was situated at 1 Soho Square, London.

THE IDEAL FOOT
SMALL IS BEAUTIFUL

When talking about women, the ideal foot is small. This has always been the case, but never more so than at the turn of the nineteenth century. At this time of fine breeding, good bone structure and respectable family background, the size of a lady's foot ranked very highly among her desirable traits.

According to *The Whole Art of Dress*: 'As in China, the greatest attention is displayed to the feet…frequently in company, I heard the chief beauties singled out among good-looking individuals, were their feet; because, perhaps they are rather small and cased in a neat pump.'

Squeezing one's feet into narrow boots and slip-on shoes – as many ladies did – left a woman with pinched feet, toes folded over each over, bunions and corns. And yet, although painful and a hindrance to walking, the fashion for tiny shoes (and a lady's adherence to that fashion) certainly created the illusion of a small, neat, feminine foot.

MARRIAGE PROSPECTS
In some circles, small feet were a prerequisite for a good marriage. A large foot was deemed too masculine and interpreted as a sign of independence and intellect – both unbecoming qualities in a woman. Ultimately big feet foreshadowed a life of spinsterhood. The Victorian writer Mary Merrifield, in *Dress as a Fine Art*, complained of 'poets and romance writers' who encouraged women to 'pinch[ed] their feet into small shoes' (1854).

Of course, the prized small foot is also evident in the story of Cinderella by Charles Perrault. Cinderella's foot is indeed small and, despite trials and tribulations, enables the girl to finally capture her prince. In contrast the ugly sisters with their huge feet will never lure a husband.

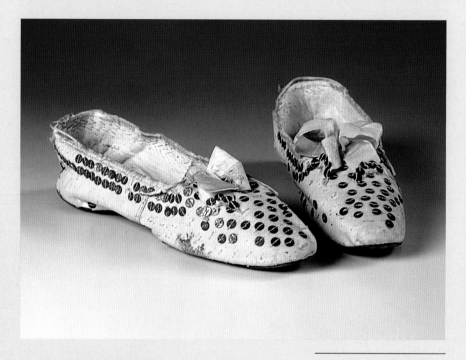

A LIFE INDOORS
While men's footwear became more comfortable and practical, enabling a man to dominate outdoor spaces, women's footwear – so delicate and impractical – confined a lady to indoors. Wearing uncomfortable footwear was a sign of social standing: the wearer couldn't walk around very much and therefore was neither able nor expected to work.

Small-sized shoes did much to show off the skill and craftsmanship of the shoemaker. Catherine Ormen-Corpet, in her *Almanach des Modes*, notes: 'With these shoes, large feet look normal, and normal feet become remarkable by the grace of their smallness' (1814–30).

ABOVE: Girls' ivory wool, slip-on shoes, 1820–9. They have a distinct square toe and are decorated with silver sequins that were originally in rows.

BELOW: Women's bronze kid leather and silk court shoes with silk-embroidered vamps and ruched silk edging, 1860s. The shoes have knock-on heels and were made by T E Moseley & Co, Boston.

CHINESE FOOT BINDING

Chinese foot binding is the ultimate in achieving the ideal small foot. This was the custom in which young girls' toes were broken and tightly bound to restrict growth over a period of time. The idea was to create a 7.5 cm (3 in) 'lotus foot'. As shown here, lotus shoes typically had triangular soles to emphasize the effect. A woman whose feet had not been bound would have difficulty finding a husband.

PROMOTING SHOES

The Industrial Revolution that began in Britain, and subsequently swept through Europe, had little impact on the shoe trade in terms of mechanization – that came later, during the 1850s. But the introduction of the railway system helped manufacturers transport their goods across Europe. It also led to the realization among shoemakers that it was time to advertise their wares.

THE ADVENT OF THE WAREHOUSE

By the last quarter of the eighteenth century, shoemakers were not only making bespoke footwear for a select clientele, but also ready-mades for an increasingly prosperous mass market. Shoe warehouses began to appear, either as sales outlets for single shoemakers or as places in which multiple shoemakers could store and sell their products through agents and distributors.

TRADE CARDS AND SHOE LABELS

This shift was coupled with a shoemaker's awareness that, in order to reach a wider audience, he needed to promote his wares. Towards the middle of the eighteenth century, many shoemakers began to circulate trade cards – a cross between a business card and an advertisement – and, in around 1750, paper labels started to appear on one of the socks inside a pair of shoes.

A label recorded the shoemaker's name (as an individual or as a small company employing other shoemakers beneath him), his location and address. For example: 'Edward Hogg Ladies Cheap Shoe Warehouse, 25 Jermyn Street, St James's, London' (c. 1800). These labels indicate that mass-produced ready-mades were competing with, if not overtaking,

bespoke shoes. They were certainly popular with the merchant classes or those with money who could go and browse the cheaper goods on offer. The bespoke shoemakers were not amused and accused warehouses of damaging their trade and of providing inferior footwear, but in the face of popular demand and the warehouse's intransigence, there was little they could do.

A label had another function. Not only did it provide a way for a shoemaker to promote himself, it also offered a means of showing off and of being acknowledged for one's shoemaking skills and craftsmanship. Shoemakers were proud of what they made. A name put to a pair of shoes also indicated a certain amount of acknowledged responsibility and comeback. Customers who were dissatisfied with their shoes could return them.

ABOVE: A nineteenth-century trade card for an English manufacturer, William Jones. Stafford was a major shoe manufacturing centre and the local MP Richard Brinsley Sheridan would use the following toast: 'May the trade of Stafford be trod under foot by all the world.'

OPPOSITE: A paper label for Melnotte, French-made shoes, c. 1827. They are on the sock of a bright pink satin, slip-on shoe with ribbon ties. They also have small labels 'droit' and 'gauche' (right and left).

6

MECHANIZATION OF THE INDUSTRY

1850s TO THE 1890s

THE FIRST FACTORIES

The second half of the nineteenth century witnessed some of the most significant changes to the shoe industry to date. The invention and development of specialized shoemaking machinery saw the establishment of the first truly modern factories in the United States and Europe – built for purpose and able to house the latest machinery. With increased output came the need for improved marketing strategies, and this gave rise to the first recognizable shoe shops.

AMERICA TAKES THE LEAD

In the United States, the shoe industry expanded on an unprecedented scale during the Civil War years of the 1860s. New, efficient factories with purpose-built machinery opened in order to meet the increased demand for military footwear. Similar working practices in Europe were inevitable and, in the 1880s, UK factory owners crossed the Atlantic to take notes on US operations and business acumen. In the United Kingdom, despite initial resistance from shoemakers, who were used to working in their own ways and to their own rhythms, the progression to working in a factory could not be halted. By the 1880s, European shoemaking industries were feeling the full force of the influence from the United States.

DEVELOPMENTS IN EUROPE

In France, François Pinet, head of the Sociétiés des Compagnons Cordonniers (Workers' Association of Shoemakers), opened his first shoe factory in Paris as early as 1855, manufacturing women's shoes. In 1863 he built a new factory at 44 rue Paradis Poissonnié, employing 120 people and with a further seven hundred men and women as outworkers. Pinet, along with other shoemakers and factory owners, oversaw the profession's move from a craft industry to a factory working on a much larger scale. Here, as well as in other European shoemaking centres – such as Northampton in England – the hand processes involved in making a shoe rapidly mechanized and those men and their families who were accustomed to creating hand-sewn footwear were swallowed up by factories. The industrial system was here to stay and influenced the style and quantity of the footwear produced.

SHIFTING INFLUENCES

In terms of fashion, the French flooded English and US markets for much of the first half of the nineteenth century, but that was set to change. English and US factories made their own 'French'-style shoes and the United States looked set to dominate from the 1850s on. This was also a time of great invention and innovation, celebrated by the Great Exhibitions of 1851 and 1862 and the 1889 Paris Exposition.

The effects of mechanization were also influencing shoemakers farther afield. Early in the 1800s, shoemakers began to establish themselves and their craft in Sydney, Australia. Many of these shoemakers had emigrated from other countries, particularly England. An easily transferable skill, written reports claim that '[by] 1828 shoemaking was after carpentry, the largest occupation, with one shoemaker per 236 inhabitants'. In the face of stiff competition in the 1880s and 1890s from US imports, federal tariff legislation of 1902 put an end to such imports and Australia's shoe industry survived well into the twentieth century.

FROM HAND-SEWN TO FACTORY-MADE

Before the industry became mechanized, individual shoemakers – perhaps with the aid of their wives and children – operated in small towns or villages where they made hand-sewn footwear for the local market. In large cities, firms operated with several shoemakers working together under one roof.

Thomas Dekker's play *The Shoemaker's Holiday* (1599) spotlights the London firm of Simon Eyre. In it the firm is run on clear divisions of labour in which each shoemaker undertook one operation for each of a small number of shoes (say ten to twelve) before passing the batch on to the next shoemaker, who carried out the next stage in the process.

Until the mid-nineteenth century, developments in England had seen contracts issued to groups of shoemakers to provide boots – for example – for the Civil War and, by 1746, the establishment of country shoe warehouses, stocking shoes from a variety of different sources. In most towns, however, shoes were still made by outworkers working at home. A manufacturer would oversee them and collect their shoes for storage in a warehouse. This type of working arrangement changed with the introduction of new, large machinery and the inevitable advent of the factory.

Among the new machines was the Singer sewing machine, exported all over Europe from the United States. Initially used to sew cloth, the machine was modified in 1856 to sew leather, so enabling the stitching together of shoe uppers. Protests from shoemakers that machines could not replicate their skills fell on deaf ears. Another American import, the Blake Sewer was, by 1864, able to stitch soles onto shoes.

While the Singer machine could be used on a domestic scale, the Blake Sewer could not. It was huge and heavy – too expensive to purchase, too big to have at home – and it needed power to run. Factory owners had the financial backing and infrastructure to house such machinery, as well as the necessary overhead belting needed to power it, initially by steam and eventually on electricity. It was this machine that forced shoemakers into factories.

STRUGGLING TO ADAPT

The transition from the home to the factory was not a smooth one. Proud craftsmen were not keen to lose their autonomy and independence. Many struggled to adapt to fixed working hours, supervision and the complete unfamiliarity of the factory environment. Working relationships also shifted as manufacturers became increasingly divorced from their employees. Foremost businessmen, rather than artisans in craft, they were less able to empathize with their workers' needs.

Although workers may have met these changes with scepticism the transition from home working to mechanization was promoted by factory owners and health officials, who argued that factories would be 'healthy, commodious and well vented apartments'.

'You will be able to eat, sleep and sit at your firesides free from the smell of the materials of manufacturing'.

Appeal from the Manfield factory.

BELOW: Men's black patent leather military dress shoe, 1828, with a square, duckbill toe and straps to lace over a high tongue. The sock has an attached label that reads 'Baywall, Dublin'. An inscription inside the shoe reads '81028 Lieut Norbury'.

FACTORY LIFE
TOURING A SHOE FACTORY

Shoe factories developed along similar lines across Europe. They required space for the two hundred or so processes involved in making a pair of shoes. On the whole, they were several storeys high and had many windows to let in much-needed light. Each department occupied its own area or level within the building. Machinery was imported from the United States, the leading nation in terms of technological developments.

Clicking (see below) tended to take place on the upper floor and closing on the floor below. Processes requiring heavy machinery were on the ground floor. From this time on, boot- and shoemaking traditionally became divided into five main stage-driven departments.

THE CLICKING ROOM
The clickers were the 'gentlemen' shoemakers. Their role involved cutting shoe uppers from the precious fine leathers, using knives with very sharply pointed blades. This highly skilled role became known as 'clicking' because the concentration required to carry out the task demanded such absolute silence that the only noise audible was the click, click, click of the blade piercing leather and hitting the wooden cutting board beneath.

THE CLOSING ROOM
Traditionally, closing was a task undertaken by a shoemaker's wife. It was only natural, therefore, that the closing room of the factory became a female environment. The closing room received the uppers – once cut out by the clickers – and around thirty operatives set about completing the numerous processes required before the shoe could be stitched together. These processes involved marking stitching lines and 'skiving' (reducing the thickness of edges where they were to form seams). Then came lining marking – which involved recording the size, fitting, last and shoe numbers on the quarter lining. Other processes might involve perforation for decorating the uppers, gimping (the serration of an edge), edging, binding and inserting eyelets. For the standard factory hours the women in the closing room earned between nine and eighteen shillings (£42.50–95/$72–144) a week, being paid 'by the piece' – where an employee is paid a fixed rate for each unit of production

THE ROUGH STUFF ROOM
This room dealt with the components commonly called 'bottom stock'. This included the cutting of the heels and soles, and those parts of the shoe that cannot be seen after construction, such as the welts. The name 'rough stuff ' may not clearly imply the skill involved in creating the foundation of the shoe, but it was a skilled job nonetheless.

THE MAKING OR LASTING ROOM
Here the soles and uppers were joined together using a foot-shaped last. The insole was attached to the last using tacks. The damp upper was then stretched over the last using a pulling-over machine and tacked to the insole. The upper fitted tightly over the last and, once dried, retained its shoe shape. A narrow strip of leather (the welt) was stitched to both the insole and the upper. To level the

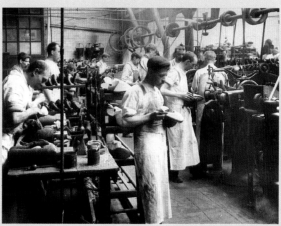

FAR LEFT: The closing room at Manfield & Sons' factory, Northampton, c. 1900

LEFT: The making room at Manfield & Sons' factory, Northampton, c. 1900.

uneven underside of the shoe, it was filled with a resin and cork mixture. It was at this stage that toe puffs, stiffeners and shanks were also added. Next the sole was stitched to the upper using the Blake Sewer. The stitches passed through the welt and sat in a channel in the sole. Finally the heel was fastened in place with nails.

THE FINISHERS

Finishers undertook the processes of trimming, smoothing and finally colouring and polishing the heel. The finishing processes were numerous and increasingly complex during this time and, as such, the finishing room was one of the last areas to become mechanized. Processes included inserting the sock inside the shoe to cover the insole, attaching any trimmings, threading laces and stamping the shoes with size information and other labels.

· By the turn of the twentieth century, the finishing room had machines for heel and edge finishing, edge setting, bottom scouring, and heel and bottom padding. All of these replaced processes previously completed by hand.

BOXING ROOM

Once all the processes had been completed, the shoes ended up in the boxing room for a final check and polish before being placed in their boxes. They were then transported across the country and exported to the rest of the world.

LEFT: The packing department at a shoe factory in Kettering, Northamptonshire, c. 1900.

RIGHT: Man's factory-made leather, ankle-high derby boot with a low-stacked heel, c. 1890. The boot has an oval toe and the toecap is edged with a line of punching. The boot is front-lacing over a bellows tongue with eight pairs of eyelets and a leather lace. Manufactured by Manfield & Sons, Northampton.

THE RISE OF AMERICA

A loss of skilled shoemakers during the War of Independence led to an immediate shortage of shoes for the US home market. This coincided with a boom in the French shoemaking industry and France began exporting on an unprecedented scale. By the 1820s, manufacture was so prolific that French ready-mades dominated both the UK and US markets.

Simple, square-toed, flat-soled, slip-on shoes with ribbon ties in black, cream and white characterized the French exports during this period. They often included a small label or ink stamp indicating *gauche* and *droit* (left and right). The French literally flooded the market with these shoes, churning them out in the thousands because they were so simple to make. The knock-on effect was particularly bad for British shoemakers, who faced reduced orders and low wages. The solution was to make French-style shoes of their own.

AMERICA ADVANCES

The Americans developed their own solution, too. Seeking processes that would increase production at a much faster rate than their slow-paced craftsmanship allowed, US shoemakers replaced the traditional iron rivet with a wooden peg. Pegging speeded up the process considerably. According to Al Saguto in *The Wooden Shoe Peg*, one could 'peg a woman's boot in as little as seven seconds' (1968). Pegs were also more suitable in the wet as, unlike their iron counterparts, they did not rust.

Used alongside stitching, and sometimes nailing, shoe-pegging became the fastest technique for attaching soles and heels to an upper part. Fast workers could finish four pairs of pegged shoes in a day, using wooden pegs made cheaply by machine. The pegs were 1.9 cm (¾ in) long, tapered and slightly thicker than a wooden match. Pegging was a skill that a young man could learn in just a few months. As such, the technique posed a threat to the traditional route of undergoing a long apprenticeship with subsequent training through experience to become a skilled shoemaker.

With industrial advancement gaining ground, the Americans established factories unhindered by tradition and were quick to assimilate emerging mechanical processes. It meant that not only did the Americans see off the French, but also the British. The British Empire grew under Queen Victoria and shoemakers had the opportunity to provide shoes to new markets in Canada, South Africa and Australia, yet they failed to compete with the rapidly changing industry in the United States. In 1893 the United Kingdom imported 2,098 dozen pairs from America. At the United States' peak in 1905, the United Kingdom imported 90,239 dozen pairs. In contrast, exports from the United Kingdom to the United States only started in 1911 with a mere 33,848 dozen pairs.

OPPOSITE LEFT: Man's python skin leg boot, made by Mahrenholz of New York, c. 1870–9. It was probably made for the centennial exhibition held in Philadelphia in 1876.

MOCCASINS

The moccasin is one of the earliest styles of footwear. Originally worn by the indigenous peoples of North America and Canada, they were traditionally made from deerskin – usually a single piece per shoe. These moccasins are made of soft leather with a velvet cuff, and are decorated with a glass bead design. Traditionally women embellished the moccasins they made with porcupine quills. These moccasins are First Nations Cree, and are dated around 1875–1900.

ABOVE: An advertisement from a catalogue for Sorosis Shoes, Lynn, Massachusetts, United States, 1901.

THE SPARKES HALL BOOT
ELASTICATED COMFORT

The beginning of the nineteenth century saw women in flat-soled, silk or satin, slip-on shoes – pretty and delicate, but impractical for anything other than a sedentary life. By the 1850s women had caught up with men's passion for boots, and one of the most popular was an elastic-sided boot that had its origins in England.

EARLY DAYS

In 1837 one Joseph Sparkes Hall, after a great deal of experimentation, presented a prototype pair of side-gusset boots to the British Queen, Victoria. The gusset was made from tiny cotton-covered brass springs, which produced the effect of being elasticated. The shoes were an early version of what was to become the elastic-sided boot, known as the congress boot and the garibaldi boot in the United States. Such boots fitted snugly around the ankle and could be pulled on and off with relative ease. The brass springs proved to be a disaster in reality, but Sparkes Hall eventually found a satisfactory solution using elastic webbing.

In his book, *The Book of the Feet*, Sparkes Hall writes: 'My first experiments were a failure…and the necessary elasticity could not be gained in any material I could meet with' (1847). Later he recorded, 'After several experiments in wire and India-rubber I succeeded in getting the exact elasticity required'.

ROYAL APPROVAL

The pair of boots that had initially been presented to Queen Victoria were well received and the queen took to wearing them frequently. This did much to increase their popularity on a wider scale. Sparkes Hall wrote: 'She walks in them daily and thus gives the strongest proof of the value she attaches to the invention'.

By 1846 the Sparkes Hall boot was incredibly popular and worn by men, women and children. Their originator was now promoting the boots with a 'cloth top and black patent toe cap'. These followed the style of the day, with square toes and flat, later low-stacked, heels.

OPPOSITE: Women's black silk and jersey elastic-sided boots, 1863–9, with patent leather, square toecaps. The boots are ankle length with U-shaped elastic gussets and have tape tabs at both front and back for pulling the boots on. A label inside reads: 'J Sparkes Hall 308 Regent Street'.

'These boots are the comfort of my life, if you were only to give them a sounding name – if you like, call them lazy boots and turn it into Greek – all the world will buy them and you'll make your fortune.'

One satisfied customer.

WOMEN'S BOOTS

The second half of the nineteenth century witnessed several new styles of boots designed specifically for women, partly in response to Queen Victoria's adoption of the Sparkes Hall boot (see pp. 112–13).

The US *Habits of Good Society: a Handbook for Ladies and Gentlemen* states that, 'It was formerly thought ungenteel to wear anything but thin Morocco shoes, or very slight boots for walking…Victoria has assumed the Balmoral petticoat… she has courageously accompanied it with the Balmoral boot…With these…the high born lady may enjoy the privileges which her inferiors possess – she may take a good walk with pleasure and safety' (1859).

The Adelaide boot was popular early on. This was a side-lace boot with a cloth top, no heel and a patent toecap. By the 1840s, the Adelaide made way for the elastic-sided boot. A fashion for steel-framed, crinoline hoop skirts that tended to swing when walking made the boot a wardrobe necessity, as they prevented a woman's ankle from becoming exposed.

From the 1860s, the front-lacing Balmoral – a closed-fronted ankle boot with a galosh – became the boot of choice. The popularity and name of this style stems from 1852, when Queen Victoria bought Balmoral Castle in Scotland. Some claim that the style was introduced by Prince Albert, who is said to have liked the boot for its slenderizing effect. Queen Victoria herself declared in 1862: 'The small boots entirely made of kid, stitched in white, laced or buttoned up the front, are in the best taste.'

THE BUTTON BOOT

For many, the boot that typifies this period is the classic button boot, which (for the elite classes) was an elegant, fitted ankle boot with scalloped buttonhole edging. For the less wealthy classes, the style was a more practical straight-up-and-down legged boot.

However presented, all button boots needed a button hook to enable the wearer to pass the buttons through the eyelets. The user inserted the tool – a steel length with a hook at one end and a handle at the other – through the eyelet and hooked it around the button. The user could then pull the button through the eyelet. With as many as twenty-five buttons per boot, the style guaranteed a neat fastening. Naturally, those who could afford it paid a maid to fasten their boots for them.

KELLY & Co.

Ladies' very fine Glace Kid
Button and Lace Boot.

BLACK
or
TAN

Fittings
3 and 4.

No. 6266.

With smart Louis XV. heels.

These heels are formed from a solid block of hard leather, ingeniously protected with a thin metal plate.

Price **17/6**

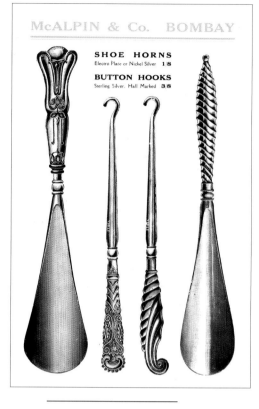

McALPIN & Co.   BOMBAY

SHOE HORNS
Electro Plate or Nickel Silver 1/8
BUTTON HOOKS
Sterling Silver. Hall Marked 3/8

DEVELOPMENTS IN THE UNITED STATES

Women in the United States were slower than their European counterparts when it came to wearing boots. The Balmoral, side- and front-lacing boots, and the Sparkes Hall boot (known as the congress or garibaldi) could all be found in the United States, though early examples from the 1840s and 1850s are rare survivors.

Between 1835 and 1860, gaiter boots were very popular. These were a side-lacing cloth boot with leather foxing. Foxing was a US term for a piece of leather that covered the lower part of a shoe or boot at the heel or toe. Gaiter boots were known as such because the leather toe and heel cap made the footwear look like gaiters. The term originally described a side-lacing style and, later, an elastic-sided boot seen by the end of the 1840s. In the 1860s, leather front-lacing boots – and subsequently button boots – were worn for walking. As US fashion magazine *The Demorest's Monthly* stated in 1883, 'Button boots are the undisputed rulers of the shoe kingdom'.

ABOVE LEFT: This advertisement appeared in the catalogue of Kelly & Co, 59 Oxford Street, London, 1903.

ABOVE RIGHT: An advertisement from the catalogue of McAlpin & Co, Civil and Military Boot Manufacturers, Bombay (now Mumbai), India, *c.* 1910.

RIGHT: Women's stylish, kid leather button boots. This pair is calf high, each with eighteen buttons. They were made in Vienna, Austria, c. 1920, and are very much in the style of the mid-1800s..

THE COURT SHOE

Although women's boots were incredibly prolific during this period, new styles of shoes developed, too. The simple, flat-soled, square-toed, ribbon-tied shoes of the first half of the nineteenth century gradually evolved into what we now call a court shoe.

Toe shapes remained squared and shallow initially, but gradually became more pointed as the period progressed. Having been quite low during the 1850s, heels rose to 6.35 cm (2½ in) in the 1860s.

VAMP EMBELLISHMENTS

Skirt fronts fell close to the body during the 1870s and 1880s, making the toes and vamps of shoes and boots more visible. Shoes therefore took on more detail in the form of punch-work, embroidery, inserts or bows.

Decorative elements on the vamp included rosettes and bows. The tiered, multi-looped fénelon bow was especially popular from around 1863. Sometimes plain, it might also be decorated with a small buckle. In the United States, court shoes were known as pumps or slippers. Evening slippers grew to large proportions in the US and finally extended up and over the top of the shoe, covering the instep. From the 1870s the style was known as the Marie Antoinette slipper.

The barrette shoe was a popular style with narrow bars of leather or textile across the instep. These were worn as both day and evening wear, and could be decorated with some sort of glass or metal beading. In 1893 Queen Mary's going-away shoe was a bronze, kid leather barrette model, decorated with a design in dull gold embroidery thread.

Common also were low, bronze, kid leather slip-on shoes with contrasting silk embroidery on the vamps. The United States's *Godey's Lady's Book* suggested a 'bronze kid slipper with appliqué pattern in blue silk and chain stitch, blue satin bow' (1855).

A CALL FOR MORE ROBUST SHOES

Women's shoes were still impractical on the whole, not suited to outdoor wear or inclement conditions. By the 1860s women were demanding more practical and hard-wearing footwear. In the United Kingdom, the *English Woman's Magazine* noted that 'Ladies have most sensibly adopted thick boots and shoes, instead of the "brown paper" soles of forty years ago' (1867).

ABOVE: Women's satin court-style shoes with a mock buckle. Made by Pattison, London, 1850s.

NEW INNOVATIONS

During the first half of the nineteenth century, the Napoleonic Wars had harnessed machinery in order to make much-needed army boots. With industrialization now underway, manufacturers began to explore further the potential of the technology at their disposal. This time of invention and innovation saw the discovery and use of a wide range of new materials and the development of advanced manufacturing processes.

RIVETING AND PEGGING

Already as early as 1810, French-born engineer Marc Isambard Brunel (father of the great English engineer, Isambard Kingdom Brunel) patented a sole-riveting machine that enabled boots to be riveted easily. A man of many talents, Brunel's brush with shoemaking may be attributed to an experience he had in Portsmouth, on the south coast of England, in 1809. Watching the surviving soldiers disembark after the Battle of Corunna during the Napoleonic Wars, he saw 'their lacerated feet wrapped in filthy rags, or partly protruding from the wretched remains of shoes'. Brunel set up a factory in Battersea, London, with machines in a production line and produced boots for the British Army.

In 1853 Thomas Crick of Leicester, England, patented his own faster, more economical method of riveting boots. In his method, wooden lasts were fitted with iron plates, which enabled the use of iron rivets instead of wooden pegs for attaching soles to uppers. Crick's was a timely development that achieved great success in the Crimean War of 1853–6.

In 1833 Samuel Preston of Danvers, Massachusetts, in the United States patented his pegging machine. Pegged footwear rapidly gained ground in the US from the 1840s (see p. 110) and is generally credited as 'essentially an American invention' (St Crispin, January 1870).

see pp. 30–1

VELDTSCHOEN CONSTRUCTION

In 1860 the Jeyes patent for stitching onto an outflanged upper was registered. This became known as Veldtschoen construction. In fact, this type of construction – also known as a 'stitch-down' construction – is very old, having been used to construct the pointed toes of medieval poulaines (see pp. 30–1). The process, which originated in South Africa, involves turning the shoe upper outwards around its bottom edge to form a flange, which is then stitched to a sole or middle sole. The Veldtschoen name appears to have been introduced into the United Kingdom as a result of the Boer War of 1899–1902, in which the Afrikaners wore shoes of untanned hide made without nails. Today the construction method is often used to make boots or shoes more waterproof for sports and outdoor activities.

ABOVE: A page from the *Fine Footwear* catalogue of the Palmer Shoe Store, Proprietors Nelson and Sargent, 541 Congress St., Portland, Maine, United States, c. 1883.

TECHNOLOGICAL MILESTONES

1830 India rubber introduced, giving rise to India rubber soles, elastic loops instead of ribbon ties and pairs of rubber galoshes.

1823 Metal eyelets patented by Thomas Rogers. They were used for stays, bodices and, of course, on boots.

1860s Metal shanks appeared, to reinforce the weak sole.

1865 Lacing hooks patented.

1865 Ooze leather introduced – an early form of suede;

1885 Box calf leather introduced. Treated with chromium salts, box calf leather had a very fine grain.

CONCEALED SHOES
HIDDEN FOR SOMEONE ELSE TO FIND

Concealed shoes are items of footwear deliberately hidden in buildings. This ancient practice raises many questions that cannot – and some argue, should not – be answered. To many, concealed shoes remain a fascinating subject and the nature of the finds (that the majority of the shoes are from poorer groups in society) is important to any student of social history. They represent types of footwear that have rarely survived in any other form.

Finds of this nature most often occur when works and renovations take place in old buildings. Old and worn out shoes are found within the fabric of a building, concealed by subsequent work. The most common places of discovery are inside chimneys, behind walls, under floorboards and in roofs. Other common hiding places include bricked-up ovens and in the vicinity of doors and staircases.

MYSTERIOUS ORIGINS

No one is quite sure how this practice came about. It could be that a well worn pair of shoes is thought to take on the appearance of the wearer, moulded over time into the shape of his or her foot, and so also embodies the spirit of the wearer. Perhaps this good spirit is contained in the shoe and helps ward off evil spirits who might want to harm the house and its occupants. The locations in which the shoes are placed (chimneys and ovens represent over one-quarter of all the concealments found) seem to suggest that the shoe offers protection for the key areas of the home and also acts as a barrier for any 'openings' in the home through which evil spirits might otherwise be tempted to enter.

In some cases, the shoes have been found with other objects, for example items of clothing, bones, paper, coins and marbles. But why conceal a shoe?

The great majority (but not all) of the concealed shoes are from working-class owners, and this in itself could be the reason why the shoes were chosen for concealment. Over the centuries, shoes have been the most expensive item of clothing for families to buy. Shoes of this class would have been precious to the wearer. Furthermore, many concealed shoe finds are children's shoes. It is thought that the spirit contained in young ones' shoes was purer and much stronger, and therefore more effective if concealed.

UNANSWERED QUESTIONS

No written evidence explaining this practice has been discovered, so it remains open to interpretation. There are many unanswered questions: did the occupants of the house conceal the shoes? Maybe, but few concealed shoes date to the time of the house being built. It is more likely that workmen or builders concealed the shoes when suitable hiding places became exposed during building work. Why, in the majority of cases, are single shoes concealed (although they can be multiple singles)? Where is the other shoe? Was the concealing of one shoe part of a pact with the other shoe retained?

In England, the Northampton Museums and Art Gallery keep a register of such finds from across the UK and farther afield covering countries including the United States, Canada and Australia – specifically those countries where the practice was introduced by immigrants.

OPPOSITE: Concealed shoes are always well worn, as these two examples illustrate. They also highlight the longevity of this worldwide practice. This child's ankle shoe (left) was found in a house in Pennsylvania, United States, and dates to around 1860. It is front-lacing, with six pairs of eyelets. It is of a turnshoe construction, although most of its quarters are missing. The woman's leather footbag (right) was found concealed above the dining room ceiling of St John's College, Oxford, England. The vamp is made in two pieces, with the toecap and vamp sewn together. It is of a welted construction with an insole and one piece outsole. It has no heel. This is a very early example and dates from around 1540.

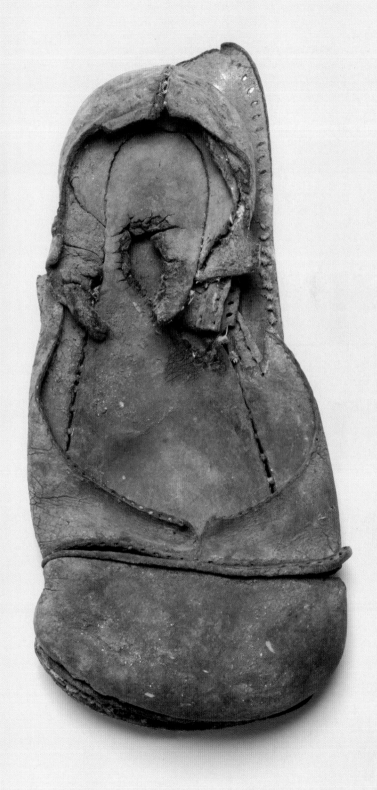

THE OXFORD AND THE DERBY

As with women's fashions, men's boots were very much in vogue during the nineteenth century. However, from around the 1840s, two classic shoe styles began to emerge: the Oxford and the Derby. These two styles went on to become the basis of many men's – and women's – shoes to the present day.

THE OXFORD

The Oxford shoe is a closed-tab, laced shoe or boot in which the eyelet tabs are stitched on the underside of the vamp. Its origins remain somewhat obscure, although some sources suggest they were first seen in Scotland and Ireland. In 1825 the men's Oxonian half-boot appeared. Originally with side slits, it developed into a side-lacing boot and, subsequently, a front-lacing shoe. Its name derives from England's Oxford University, where the style was widely adopted by students during the first half of the nineteenth century. In 1846 J Sparkes Hall informed us in *The New Monthly Magazine* that 'Dress pumps are the only shoes now worn. The Oxonian shoe…is the best for walking. It laces up the front with three or four holes. It is none other than high lows now called Oxford shoes'.

The Oxford style was seen in the United States from the 1870s onwards, where it was known as a Balmoral or Bal-type shoe. President Thomas Jefferson wore Oxfords despite being accused of foppishness. In Italy, Berlutti were known as the makers of exquisite men's Oxfords at the turn of the twentieth century. Brogue Oxfords were made by Gatto, also in Italy, at the beginning of the twentieth century, and could be bought in the big US shoe shops, including Florsheim, established in 1892.

LEFT: An enduring and classic style, this leather Derby shoe was manufactured by Barker, Earls Barton, Northamptonshire, c. 1992.

THE DERBY

The Derby is a laced boot or shoe in which the eyelet tabs are stitched on top of the vamp. It almost certainly developed from the Blucher army boot (see p. 92) and was sometimes referred to as a Blucher in the United States. While the Oxford usually has two lines of stitching, or similar decoration, across the toe, the Derby is usually plain.

The first mention of the name Derby as a style term for footwear is in Dunkley's account book of 1862 where the term describes a pair of side sprung boots – though this is no longer in keeping with the shoe we associate with the name today. The shoe was also known as a Gibson in the United States, as well as a Blucher, and across Europe by the French name, the Molière.

'The Derby a new tie shoe better than the Oxonian as the seam is not near the tender part of the foot.'

St Crispin's Magazine, 1872.

BELOW: A rival to the Derby, this is a lovely example of the classic Oxford shoe, 1890–1910. It has an oval toe with a low-stacked heel and was manufactured by Craddock Bros Ltd, Bootmakers, Wolverhampton.

SLIPPERS

With the latest fashions primarily centred on boots for outdoor wear throughout much of this period, etiquette required a change of shoe for indoors. For both men and women this meant a rise in popularity for the indoor slipper. One of the most endearing slipper styles at the time was the elegant, backless mule. Such fashions came from Paris, which remained the centre of European fashion until the Franco-Prussian War in 1870.

LADIES' STYLES

The term 'slipper' does not refer, as today, to comfortable, cosy footwear for cold, winter evenings, but rather a style of indoor footwear that is more akin to boudoir slippers – generally more delicate, less bulky and extremely feminine. For the most part, slippers would have been worn in private in the bedroom or for partaking of breakfast within a family setting. As they became more widely worn, the American bible of good taste, *Godey's Lady's Book*, declared: 'Dressing slippers are well in their way; and often daintily becoming. It is never well to be without a pair, in your bag or basket, for your state-room or the hotel; but a slippered foot, descending from a rail car, or promenading a deck, however pretty and attractive, would be very likely to subject the owner to impertinent, if not unkind remark and criticism' (July 1857).

The backless mule or boudoir slipper of this period is perfectly illustrated by French artist Edouard Manet's portrait *Olympia* (1863), in which Olympia is a nude prostitute. She lies propped up by cushions – nude apart from her jewellery, hair ornament and…a pair of mules.

MEN'S STYLES

Slippers for men were also common, although they were rather more like contemporary men's slippers, comfort being one of the main requirements. The basic style was a tabbed-fronted, slip-on shoe, often worked in a Berlin wool design, tapestry or kilim weave.

In England, this style became known as the Albert slipper (after Prince Albert), in which the vamp extended upwards to form a tongue resting on the instep. The Albert slipper was usually made from black velvet with a quilted lining and leather sole. It was the epitome of domestic relaxation. You could even get the style in Berlin woolwork or, for the ultimate indulgence, monogrammed with your initials.

LEFT: A page from a catalogue for slippers by Manfield & Sons', Northampton, c. 1905.

OUTDOOR FOOTWEAR

The late nineteenth century was very much the period for men wearing boots for out-of-doors pursuits, and a good number of styles were available to the discerning gentleman. The wellington, the hessian and the Blucher, all of which had their origins in the late eighteenth and early nineteenth centuries, continued to be popular (see pp. 92–5). English men also wore a form of Sparkes Hall boot (see pp. 112–13).

A style called the Albert emerged during this time. It had a closed-tab galosh that was ankle high, with five buttons (sometimes mock buttons) coupled with an elastic side or side-lace fastening. There was also a style called a high-low, described by the writer Robert Bloomfield in his poem *The Farmer's Boy* as 'a covering for the foot and ankle too high to be called shoe and too low for a boot' (1801). He also mentions them in a letter to his friend Mary Lloyd Baker, where he notes 'a high-low or high boot, very ponderous, and filled with nails in the heel' (25 March 1807), which was

thrown at someone to wish him good luck on his journey. Illustrations show such boots to be front-laced with an open tab. Originally worn by country folk, high-lows also had hobnail soles and plated heels. In general, boots had fairly low-stacked heels – 3 cm (1–1¼ in) high. Toes were quite narrow and long, although by the 1880s there was a rise in popularity for a pointed toe, culminating in the American-influenced toothpick toe – pointed and upturned.

THE COWBOY BOOT

Cowboys herding cattle needed an appropriate boot, one that would slip into the stirrup easily and with a low heel to keep it in place. It also had to be made from thick leather extending up the leg to protect the wearer from natural hazards such as rattlesnakes and cactus thorns, plus possible chafing from the saddle and horse. Apparently in 1870, John Cubine of Coffeyville, Kansas, took the original design further by combining the wellington with the military boot to create the iconic cowboy style with a high top and Cuban heel.

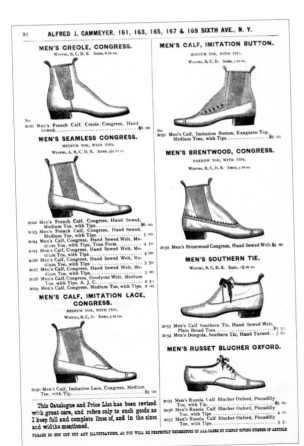

FAR LEFT: A page from an illustrated catalogue of Alfred J Cammeyer, 161–169 Sixth Avenue, New York, in the United States.

LEFT: A photograph of King Edward VII of England, by W and D Downey, taken on 1 January 1892. He wears knickerbockers above his front-lacing ankle boots.

BELOW: A man's crocodile
leather Blucher or Derby boot,
1870s–80s.

No. 1239
16/6

No. 1032—
16/6

Willow Calf
Derby Boot.

Also in Box Calf

No. 1501
10/6

GENTLEMEN'S BOOTS for Town Wear.

For Gentlemen who require a
boot to stand exacting wear.

Strong Box Calf, with
medium-stout sole.

Also in Brown Willow

No. 1024—
10/6

Smart Light Glace Kid Boot.
Very special value.

Also in Patent Calf

Strong Reliable Boot in Box Calf.
The most popular of our Half-guinea Lines.

ABOVE: A page from a
catalogue of Manfield & Sons'
Boots, Northampton, c. 1905.
The company claims that:
'Manfield's boots include a
style for every requirement
and as many shapes, fittings
and half sizes…They are worn
by all classes of the public,
and there is a boot or shoe
provided to meet the needs of
each wearer and the demands
of every occasion.'

THE PLIMSOLL

The introduction of India rubber in the 1830s made a significant impact on the development of what we now know as the trainer or sneaker. During the first half of the nineteenth century, American Charles Goodyear spent years studying the properties of rubber, eventually inventing a heating process called vulcanization in 1839.

The process transformed rubber into a tough and reliable material, as opposed to a product that would turn sticky in hot weather and brittle in cold. In 1844 Goodyear applied for a US patent and began to make all sorts of rubber goods, including rubber-soled canvas boots.

THE GREEN FLASH

Across the Atlantic, Scotsman John Boyd Dunlop was also experimenting with rubber. Having observed the discomfort endured by his son when riding his tricycle with solid rubber tyres over cobbles, Dunlop decided to wrap the wheels in thin rubber sheets, glue them together and inflate them for a cushioning effect. He had created the pneumatic tyre. By 1927 Dunlop had joined forces with the Liverpool Rubber Co Ltd and extended their rubber range to include protective footwear, including a Dunlop wellington. In 1929 the 'green flash' Dunlop tennis shoe was introduced and worn by Fred Perry, three-time Wimbledon champion in the 1930s.

THE PLIMSOLL LINE

This new process became the basis for modern sports shoe designs. In the late 1860s a shoe with a canvas upper and rubber sole was made for summer wear. Known originally as sand shoes, Phillip Lace of the Liverpool Rubber Co Ltd renamed them 'plimsolls' in 1876. This came a year after the Plimsoll Line (named after its originator, Samuel Plimsoll) became compulsory for shipping. The term plimsoll was applied to the shoes because the coloured horizontal band joining the upper to the sole resembled the Plimsoll Line on a ship's hull. On ships, the marking indicated the waterline limit and, similarly, if water got above the line of the plimsoll's rubber sole, the wearer would get wet. The Universal Plimsoll trademark was registered on 15 May 1885.

In the May 1900 issue of the *American Shoe Retailer*, it was noted that the rubber-soled canvas shoes worn by fashionable folk for playing tennis and boating had become a uniform for the young, who performed all variety of 'stunts' in them.

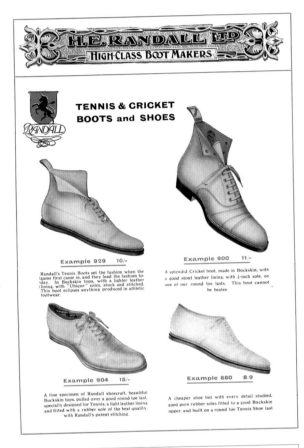

ABOVE: A page from the catalogue/price list of the Eastern Rubber Company, Proprietors Worthley, Downes & Co, 29 Milk and 2–4 Hawley Streets, Boston, Massachusetts, United States, 1880.

TOP LEFT: A page from the catalogue of H E Randall Ltd, Northampton, c. 1910, advertising tennis and cricket boots and shoes. Their footwear was exported across the world, including to India and the Far East. They also had many shops at the beginning of the twentieth century, including three in Paris, France.

BOTTOM LEFT: H E Randall Ltd were also the manufacturers of the wonderfully named 'Tenacious' tennis shoes with moulded rubber soles, 1888.

LEFT: A classic, white canvas, lace-up plimsoll with rubber soles, made by the firm Dunlop, 1920–39.

RIGHT: A woman's glacé leather, bar-strap tennis shoe with a rubber sole, 1900–20.

EXHIBITION FOOTWEAR

For a short period from the late eighteenth century to the 1860s, prize competitions were held to judge the talents of the industry's shoemaker craftsmen. These competitions often took place at the world fairs that did much to disseminate the cultural, scientific and technological developments of the great industrial age.

Quite often prize shoes were made in exaggerated forms with odd-shaped toes, excessively high heels and hand-sewn seams up to forty stitches to 2.5 cm (1 in). The shoes were not made to be worn, but to show off the shoemaker's exquisite skills. Despite mechanization – or perhaps in spite of mechanization – shoemakers continued to demonstrate their dextrous skills in this way.

WORLD'S FAIRS

Beginning with the Great Exhibition of 1851 in London, shoemakers produced amazing boots and shoes that demonstrated small stitching and complex designs. These shoes were often full size and could be worn if one was able get them on one's feet. They all show an incredibly high standard of workmanship.

High-quality footwear was also exhibited in the United States at such fairs as the 1876 Centennial Exhibition in Philadelphia and the 1893 World's Columbian Exposition in Chicago. The examples on display all showed exceptionally high levels of craftsmanship. In France, Paris exhibitions from the 1850s onwards showcased shoemakers' work – including the 1889 Exposition Universelle.

These international exhibitions provided a way of keeping handcraftsmanship very much alive in the face of widespread mechanization. They also provided an excellent way for shoemakers to promote their skills at home and abroad and to demonstrate the range of shoes available.

MINIATURES

Many shoemakers made miniature shoes in their spare time. They had access to scraps of leather and spare components and after a day's graft would sit at home making small versions of the court shoe, Oxford or Derby (see pp. 116–17, 122–3).

OPPOSITE: An exquisite pair of rust-coloured satin, lace-up boots overlaid with Chantilly lace. The boots were made by shoemaker M E Sablonniére for the Paris Exposition of 1889. Naturally he won a gold medal for his efforts.

LEFT: Winning a prize medal at the Great Exhibition of 1851, these boots exemplify the shoemaker's craftsmanship. A leather dress wellington boot, the front leg is decorated with an appliqué design in black leather and coloured silk (now missing) of a crown, national emblems, crosses, stars and a scalloped border. The back of the boot is decorated with a scrolling pattern. They were designed and made by Derby shoemakers J N Hefford and Sons, manufacturers of hand-sewn boots and importers of French shoes.

UNION ACTIVITY
UNITED WE STAND

By the nineteenth century, small, local organizations sought to protect the interests of workers over labour conditions, pay rates and hours. Among the first of these unions in the UK was the Amalgamated Cordwainers Association, founded in 1840. Its members were makers of hand-stitched shoes who resented the mass-production techniques that were emerging in the 1850s.

Over the ensuing decades, union activity of one sort or another occurred in dominant centres of the shoemaking industry. The sequence of events in Northampton – at the time, the United Kingdom's leading shoemaking centre – is just one example of events that took place in many cities throughout Europe and the United States.

THE THREAT OF THE FACTORY LOOMS

In 1857, when the first machines for shoe production appeared in Northampton, England, the town's shoemakers feared widespread unemployment – or that those managing to keep their livelihood would be forced into factories. In November of that year shoemakers held a meeting to discuss the introduction of machinery and the building of a 'monster warehouse' in the town, which they suspected would actually serve as a factory. In April 1858 the Northampton Boot and Shoemakers Mutual Protection Society was formed to oppose mechanization. A strike fund was created and links made with Stafford's shoemakers who were already engaged in a dispute over machinery.

In February 1859 Northampton manufacturers issued the following statement: 'That in consequence of sewing machines being extensively used in the Cities and Principal Towns in the United Kingdom, so as seriously to affect the demand upon the Wholesale House any further delay in the introduction of them, by the Manufacturers of Northampton, would be permanently injurious to the interest of the trade generally. And in accordance with this conviction, it was decided to introduce the Machine Sewn Tops simultaneously into their respective Trades.'

A strike was called and shoemakers were urged to leave the town and find work elsewhere. However, it transpired that shoemakers did not have strong objections to the introduction of machinery as long as they didn't lose their jobs. By 1864 fifteen thousand closing machines were in use.

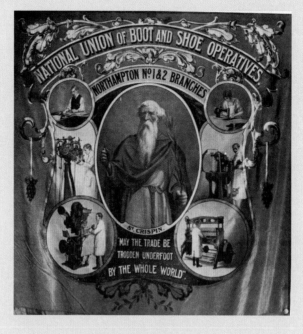

LEFT: A St Crispin banner made from silk for the Northampton Branch of the National Union of Boot and Shoe Operatives, c. 1910.

A STRIKE TO END STRIKES

In 1885 a dispute over wages resulted in the 'last strike', when 46,000 shoemakers all over the United Kingdom were involved in a lockout by the manufacturers. The Terms of Settlement that ended this strike included a 'no strike, no lock out' clause and formed the basis of industrial relations from then on. The only other major demonstration to do with wages was The Raunds March in 1905, when army bootmakers marched to London to protest against the system of tendering, which kept their wages low.

STRIKE ACTIVITY IN THE UNITED STATES

Just as in England, the introduction of mechanization threatened American shoemakers. In an attempt to regulate its use, workers organized the Knights of St Crispin. However, the climate of the time and the speed and efficiency of new machinery proved to be a very powerful opponent and ultimately one that could not be beaten.

In 1895 the largest shoe unions, along with a number of independent locals, joined to form the Boot and Shoe Workers Union (BSWU), which went on to affiliate with the American Federation of Labor in 1895. The BSWU continued to thrive until the late 1960s.

ABOVE: A Boot and Shoe Workers Union badge, c. 1910. The union was established in the United States in 1895.

LEFT: An American conference badge for the vice-president of Goodyear Shoe Operators Protective Union, c. 1920s. At the centre of the rosette, there is a picture of a man's six-button boot, around which it reads: 'Goodyear Shoe Operatives Protective Union'.

RIGHT: This man's leather Balmoral boot, 1888, is one of several held at Northampton Museum, England, that were made for the Arbitration Board after the 1887 boot and shoe industry strike. It is signed on the sole by M P Manfield (for the manufacturer) and by F Inwood (for the union).

SHOE SHOPS

The first recognizable shoe shops appeared around 1800 in fashionable shopping destinations such as London, Paris and New York. Like today, such establishments carried a wide range of footwear and had an area in which customers could try on shoes. By the middle of the nineteenth century, such shops were common in major cities and towns throughout Europe.

Following widespread mechanization, with shoes now available in larger numbers, manufacturers realized that they could make more profit if they marketed their own products. Manfield & Sons' in Northampton, England, had opened one of the first shoe factories. The firm was also among the first to open a shop, in the early 1880s. Other firms soon followed, with well-known brands soon appearing on the high street. In England these included Barratts, True-Form and Freeman, Hardy and Willis.

The same thing was happening in the United States: manufacturer Florsheim opened a shop in Chicago not long after they were established in 1894. Originally they had made shoes for other retailers to sell under their own labels, but the firm soon realized the merit of producing the shoes under their own brand name.

ABOVE: Manfield & Sons' shopfront, *c.* 1925. The firm had many shops all across the UK and farther afield in Amsterdam, Marseilles, Brussels, Hamburg and Paris – where they opened six shops alone.

ABOVE: The Ladies Showroom at 169 Regent Street, London, 1905–10, as featured in the catalogue of the American Shoe Company. The company was established for the exclusive sale of American boots and shoes. They made special arrangements with the best manufacturers in the United States for the supply of the highest grades and newest styles of ladies', gentlemen's and children's shoes and boots. The company boasted of an elevator to all floors, which they claimed was a novelty in England at the time.

'There is a large class of persons in London etc., who sell boots and shoes, but do not manufacture them. The greater part of these persons know no more how a boot or shoe is made, than the boots and shoes are said to possess such knowledge.'

J Sparkes Hall, *The Book of the Feet* (1847).

RIGHT: A pair of women's black leather court shoes with a Louis heel, a cut-out design on the vamp and decorated with black beads. They are still with their original box and were manufactured by William Hickson & Sons, of Northampton, as part of their 'Ubique' line, 1880–9.

BELOW: Shoebox labels provided a good way of promoting a brand and creating a distinctive look for individual firms. Saks box (left) c. 1950. Fine Footwear box (right) c. 1900.

CLOGS

Clogs were fairly widespread throughout Northern Europe during the nineteenth and early twentieth centuries. Primary centres of production included the north and west of England – Cumbria, Lancashire, Cheshire and Yorkshire; the Scottish border counties; the south and west of Wales; and northern European countries, in particular the Netherlands, Belgium and France.

EUROPEAN STYLES

Clogs made outside of the British Isles tended to be made entirely out of wood – the Dutch clog being the typical style. They were sometimes painted yellow or red. The French *sabot* could be all wood or with a wooden sole and leather upper. Shiny black leather uppers were also very popular. These styles of clogs tended to have quite upturned, pointed toes. Sometimes there was a leather strap across the instep to help keep the shoe on.

ENGLISH INTERPRETATIONS

English clogs typically have a leather upper, wooden sole and one of several different fastenings. The most common style was the clasp clog – in use until at least the end of the eighteenth century – in which the upper was fastened by two metal clasps that met in the middle. The bar-strap clog, with a single bar across the instep ending with a button fastening, was also popular. Generally speaking, women and girls in the textile mills wore traditional clasp clogs or bar-strap clogs, the latter becoming more popular at the beginning of the nineteenth century. Such shoes were also a popular choice for protective wear in other industrial environments such as breweries, laundries, bleach and dye works, mines, quarries and for farming.

The wood of choice for soles was alder, which was light, straight-grained, water-resistant and didn't split. Dancing clogs were usually made from ash, which gives a distinctive 'tap' sound. A variety of leathers were used for the uppers including best kip (calf, kid or lamb skin), grained and split leather. (Thick hides are usually separated into layers, where 'grained' leathers are those immediately below the animal hair, while 'split' leather refers to the layer beneath.) Clogs follow their own regional fashions and styles, with a variety of different toe shapes and incised decoration.

During construction the uppers were removed from the last and nailed to the clog sole using a narrow leather or metal strip over the join. Iron nails were usually used around the heel and on anything but the cheapest clogs, brass around the forepart. The purpose of this was to create a waterproof seal. Great care had to be taken to angle the nail in such a way that it didn't pierce the wearer's foot when wearing the shoes.

To prevent excessive wear on the wooden soles, clogs would often have shaped irons pinned to the sole and heel, rather like horseshoes. Most clogs came with these already attached, although you could purchase the clogs at a cheaper price without them and then buy the irons separately from a local blacksmith. It was not always economical to do this, however.

LEFT: Men's Dutch-style clogs. This pair has been painted yellow and made to look like button shoes. Such clogs were made well into the mid-twentieth century.

BELOW: This stylish French *sabot* in the mule style dates from the early twentieth century. It has a leather upper above carved wooden soles and heels.

BELOW: Clog design remained unchanged well into the twentieth century. This brightly coloured pair from the Netherlands dates from 1920–39.

7

THE TURN OF THE TWENTIETH CENTURY

1890s TO THE 1920s

TOWARDS A MODERN SHOE

Thanks to the promotion of ideas, craftsmanship and design at world fairs hosted across the globe from the 1850s onwards, as well as the rise of new and easily available media – from films to fashion magazines and photography – the latest developments in fashion were now within easy reach of many who had not enjoyed such access before. This coincided with the establishment of shoemaking factories producing footwear on such a wide scale that well-made shoes in the latest styles were available and affordable to almost everybody. This, coupled with a growth in outdoor pursuits, sports and the invention of the automobile, meant that there was a new emphasis on designing shoes for specific activities.

GREATER FREEDOM FOR WOMEN

The Western world was changing. By the end of the nineteenth century, European and American women were beginning to push for their rights. They wanted to pursue more active roles than public attitudes and restrictive, tight-fitting dresses had previously decreed. As early as 1881, the Rational Dress movement in England advocated styles of clothing based on ideals of 'health, comfort and beauty'. By the twentieth century, such ideas were rapidly gaining momentum, and changing lifestyles began to erode hitherto accepted ideals of a woman's role in society.

Bicycling had become popular with women from the 1890s. In the United States, Amelia Jenks Bloomer promoted the idea of women abandoning their petticoats for a trousered outfit that later became known as the bloomer. Ladies adopted these bloomers as suitable cycling wear, preferring their practical advantage over trailing skirts. Appropriate footwear evolved at the same time, with leather bicycling shoes or boots made in a sturdy yet flexible style.

AMERICAN SUCCESS

The widespread export of American mass-manufactured shoes continued well into the twentieth century, with a crippling effect on manufacturing in UK factories. The United States also began to challenge Paris as the centre for fashion. It could be said that the period from 1870 to 1930 was the heyday of American manufacturing, with millions of pairs of American-made shoes exported to Europe. Brooklyn, New York, became an important shoemaking centre – so much so that shoes manufactured there were known as 'Brooklyn Shoes'. The industry in Philadelphia was also thriving, where the company Bray Bros was renowned for its popular style, the tango, an open-laced shoe or boot. Compared to the exclusive footwear of such French shoemakers as Pinet, mass-produced American footwear was cheaper and available on a greater scale to many more people.

EUROPEAN MANUFACTURERS

In 1851 Carl Franz Bally opened a factory in Switzerland, which later made great use of new shoemaking machinery imported from the United States. By 1916 Bally were manufacturing four million pairs of shoes a year, and they were able to trade in both Europe and America during the First World War owing to their neutral position. Italy was also starting to muscle in on the world's footwear stage. Pietro Yantorney became one of the first recognized shoe designers, swiftly followed by the sartorial powerhouse of Salvatore Ferragamo. The defining event of this period was the First World War, after which women's future emancipation became inevitable and the declining fortunes of the shoe industry – in part triggered by the war – reversed.

THE RETURN OF THE HEEL

At the turn of the twentieth century, the flat-soled styles popular during the early 1800s were cast aside as the heel made a welcome comeback to women's footwear. The return of the heel had been a steady process: it rose to 1.9 cm (¾ in) in 1851, and by 1860 it was not uncommon to see shoes with heels as high as 6.3 cm (2½ in).

Among the popular styles were the Louis heel (see p. 60), the knock-on heel of around 1855 and the Pinet heel of 1867. The Pinet heel followed the Louis heel shape but was, in essence, less curvy. High, curvy heels on boots were particularly prevalent from the 1880s.

A fashion for brass heel pieces emerged towards the end of the nineteenth century (see quote). Where the report in the journal refers to the 'top piece', this actually means the base of the heel. A practical necessity in the case of the extravagantly high shoes of the 1890s – since it helped to protect and strengthen the heel – the brass heel was adopted as a fashion accessory on many shoes. Up to 6 mm (¼ in) thick, the plate was often engraved with a decorative design. Catching the light as the wearer moved about, the brass addition provided an extra fashionable element.

SHOE STYLES

The classic women's court shoe that forms the basis of many styles today became known as such during the second half of the nineteenth century (see pp. 116–17). Prior to this the name was used more frequently for footwear worn by men at the royal court or on formal occasions. In the United States, this style of low-cut, slip-on shoe with a heel is known as a pump. The style became increasingly fashionable, with advertisements in catalogues of the day exhibiting a variety of coloured and decorated court shoes.

Embroidery, a range of bows – from the simple to the extravagant fénelon bow – and beading on the uppers and, in particular, on the toes were prevalent. Such decorative elements provided an excellent way for women at home to modify and give life to an otherwise tired pair of shoes. The introduction of synthetic dyes from the 1860s onwards also meant that these shoes could take on all manner of new and exciting colours.

Increasingly sensible and practical footwear for walking and other activities was also available at this time, reflecting the changes in attitudes to women's dress. These often sported low-stacked heels as opposed to the higher carved wooden heels covered in leather or textile.

LEFT: A page from the illustrated catalogue and price list of A J Cammeyer, 161–9 Sixth Avenue, New York, United States, 1892. It shows a good range of women's court shoes, or slippers, as they are termed in America.

OPPOSITE: A woman's suede leather court shoe, painted with a floral design, c. 1900. It has a gilt Louis heel and is labelled 'Maykopf, London'.

'The latest Parisian novelty of Louis XV heels with tips showing between the top piece and the body of the heels.'

Boot & Shoe Trades Journal, October 1888.

THE CROMWELL

First seen in England in 1885, the Cromwell was a high-heeled shoe with a tabbed front and a buckle in cut steel (or later marcasite) that usually slotted onto the straps. The style was called the Cromwell in the mistaken belief – or in a late Victorian fanciful moment – that buckles had been worn on the shoes of Oliver Cromwell and his followers during the first half of the seventeenth century.

In reality, at that time Cromwell's men wore practical, low-heeled leather shoes fastened with a latchet tie. Nevertheless, the name stuck. These extremely decadent shoes have heels as high as 16 cm (6¼ in). More modest examples for the less daring had lower heels and a wider variety of fastenings.

FRENCH ORIGINS

The style had origins in the late 1860s and was also known as a Molière shoe, although the design was a modest relation when compared to these later versions. Madame de Villedieu described the French playwright Molière – with whom the name of the shoe is associated – on stage: '…his shoes were so embellished with ribbons, that it was impossible to tell whether they were Russian leather or English cowhide; anyway I am sure they were a good six inches high and I was at a loss to imagine how such a high and slender heel could hold up the marquis' ribbons, breeches, trimmings, powder and body.'

AN IMPRACTICAL CHOICE

Such an amazingly high-heeled shoe caused suitable consternation. Wearers were ridiculed and cartoons of the day apparently carried images of women needing sticks to walk or helping hands on either side of them. Towards the end of the 1890s these exaggerated heels became just the thing for women who entertained in the boudoir, thereby solving the problem of having to walk in them! Such shoes also contributed to a lady's age-old desire to make her feet look smaller than they truly were (see p. 98). Peeping out from beneath a skirt they would have created the illusion of very small, neat feet indeed. Their fashionable status teetered, and finally petered out, by 1900 – largely owing to their sheer impracticality.

ABOVE: A page from a catalogue of the American Shoe Co, 169 Regent Street, London, 1905–10. It features the company's 'La Parisienne' Cromwell-style shoes.

WHAT'S IN A NAME?

The Cromwell was one of several shoe styles towards the end of the nineteenth century to be named after a person, real or not. An open-tabbed Derby shoe with wide laces was named the Gibson after the Gibson Girl of the 1890s – a pen-and-ink cartoon representation of the perfect American girl. Also, a similar shoe to the Cromwell, though with a tie fastening, was the Langtry. This was named after actress and friend to the British monarchy, Lily Langtry.

YANTORNEY, PERUGIA AND PINET
THE WORLD'S FIRST SHOE DESIGNERS

Shoemakers have been designing shoes for centuries, driven by their own inspiration, expertise, input from patrons and the times in which they lived. Most early shoemakers were anonymous, simply admired for their skill and craftsmanship. Shoemakers' labels, introduced in the eighteenth century (see p. 100), provide a name and location, but in some cases little more.

By the end of the nineteenth century, individual names were becoming prominent, among them Pietro Yantorney, André Perugia and Jean-Louis François Pinet. One of these men – Yantorney – is frequently referred to as the world's first shoe designer. Yantorney is known as the 'elusive shoemaker' because very little is known about his personal life. Born in 1890 in Calabria, Italy, Yantorney became the curator of the shoe collection at the Cluny Museum, Paris. In 1904 he set up his own small workshop.

A part-time shoemaker, he worked only for the rich, demanding a large deposit for each pair of shoes commissioned. In return he undertook to make his clients' shoes for life. He took casts of a client's feet and watched as he or she walked around barefoot so that he could see how body weight was distributed when moving. This determined the style of shoe he made. Often, he would not see the client again until the shoes were ready – as long as three years in some cases.

The wealthy socialite Mrs Rita de Acosta Lydig was a client who commissioned Yantorney to make over three hundred pairs of shoes. Her sister recalled, 'You could count on the first pair being delivered in about two years. If he liked you very much, as he did Rita, you might hope to get them in a year, or if a miracle occurred, six months.' Mrs Lydig travelled often and had two Russian leather cases lined in cream velvet to house her shoes. To keep the shoe trees inside the case light, Yantorney made them from antique violins that Mrs Lydig bought especially. The case is now in the Metropolitan Museum of Art, New York.

PERUGIA AND PINET

Italian-born André Perugia worked in his father's workshop in Nice, France, before setting up his own operation. What better position than on the Côte d'Azur? Among his first clients was the wife of the owner of the famous Negresco Hotel on the seafront, who allowed Perugia to display and promote his shoes in the foyer. The shoes caught the eye of a wealthy client of the couturier Paul Poiret, and Poiret subsequently invited Perugia to show his shoes at Maison Poiret in Paris. Perugia went on to make shoes for Poiret as well as other Parisian fashion designers, and he opened his own shop in Paris on the rue du Faubourg Saint-Honoré. Such was his influence that Saks Fifth Avenue retailed his ready-to-wear Padova range.

Perugia's passion was for precision at all times, which meant he placed an emphasis on making shoes that not only looked breathtakingly beautiful but also fitted perfectly. Both beauty and ergonomic exactness were key. The one wouldn't work without the other. Among his clients were Pola Negri, Polish star of the silent movies, Gloria Swanson, Josephine Baker and the French actress, singer and showgirl Mistinguett, whose amazing legs enabled Perugia to show off his skills as a bespoke shoemaker.

French-born Jean-Louis François Pinet was the son of a shoemaker and learned the trade from his father. He arrived in Paris in the 1840s, opening his first factory in 1855. Pinet was renowned for his elegant shoes and exquisitely embroidered boots.

ABOVE: Women's dark red Genoese velvet shoes with gold metal thread and floral embroidered decoration, made by Yantorney, c. 1920. The Louis heel, pointed toe and extended tongue with diamanté buckle are all unmistakable characteristics of Yantorney's designs. Amazingly the shoes still have their original cherry wood shoe trees inside them marked 'L' and 'R'.

BELOW: Women's evening shoe in sumptuous red and gold leather with a richly decorated vamp. The shoes were made by André Perugia in the 1920s and sold by Saks Fifth Avenue, New York.

EARLY SPORTS FOOTWEAR

As early as 1517, King Henry VIII of England had a pair of tennis shoes in his wardrobe: 'Itm for soling of syxe paire of shooys with feltys to playe in at tenneys…' (Great Wardrobe Accounts of 1517). It would be several centuries before another pair was seen.

Rubber-soled footwear began to appear from the 1860s. At the time, the comfort and flexibility of their design made them ideal for croquet and beachwear. It was not long before similar footwear appeared for playing tennis and cricket and for running and yachting. By the end of the nineteenth century, rubber had become a major material for footwear and this, coupled with the rising popularity of sports and outdoor pursuits, saw the establishment of two of the United States' most iconic sports footwear companies, Converse and Keds.

ALL STARS

Founded by Marquis M Converse in 1908, Converse can perhaps be regarded as the United States' first original sports shoe company. The company began as a rubber shoe manufacturer, offering rubber-soled footwear for men, women and children. In 1912 the company produced a tennis shoe and, in 1917, the world's first performance-based basketball shoe – the iconic Converse All Star.

In 1918 a player from the Akron Firestones basketball team acquired his first pair of All Star shoes, introducing them (and basketball) to Americans across the country. That player was Charles H Taylor. Known as 'Chuck', Taylor officially joined Converse in 1921 as the United States' first player-endorser. Two years later, his signature appeared in the All Star patch. Converse grew in the 1930s, alongside the nation's interest in basketball. The company became synonymous with the sport and the Converse Chuck Taylor All Star became the basketball shoe of choice for professionals and high school teams throughout the country. Affectionately known as Chucks, Connies or Cons, they became a lasting American icon.

THE SNEAKER

Keds were established in 1916 by the US Rubber Company. The firm marketed its tennis shoes as sneakers and the term became synonymous with a wide range of sports shoes. The term 'sneaker' was not original at the time, however. In F W Robinson's book, *Female Life in Prison*

by a Prison Matron, we learn that 'the night officer is generally accustomed to wearing a species of India rubber shoes or galoshes on her feet' (1862). According to Robinson, these shoes are termed 'sneaks' by the female inmates of Brixton Prison, London.

Later, in 1870, North American etymologist James Greenwood registered the word 'sneaker' in reference to the quiet sound coming from shoes with rubber soles and canvas tops.

ABOVE: Marilyn Monroe and Keith Andes as Joe Doyle and Peggy during the filming of *Clash by Night*, Monterey, California, c. 1952. Both actors are clad in sports footwear.

LEFT: Natural beige, canvas and crêpe, rubber-soled hi-tops, 1924–9. These very rare, early examples of Keds sneakers were named Conquest and cost between $1 and $4 at the time.

THE CHELSEA BOOT

Changes to men's shoe fashions during this period were less dramatic than those seen in women's footwear. Boots were still very popular, especially front-lacing and button-boot styles. The side-elastic boot was also worn, usually as eveningwear. Whatever the shoe style at this time, it usually had a stacked heel that was quite low at about 3.8 cm (1½ in).

The cloth-topped button boot became popular. This combined a leather or patent upper with a cloth leg. As for many men today, the popular choice of shoe during this period was the open-tab Derby or the closed-tab Oxford (see pp. 122–3). The brogue shoe appeared around this time, sporting punched decoration that was reminiscent of earlier shoe styles (see pp. 158–9).

With origins in the Sparkes Hall boot of the 1840s (see pp. 112–13), elastic-sided boots were known as congress or garibaldi boots in the United States. In England they became known as the Chelsea boot. The earliest use of the name 'Chelsea' occurs in a late 1860s price list by a firm called Wasers, who advertised men's, women's and boy's Chelsea boots. Why the name Chelsea? Sadly, the exact origins of the term are unknown. One suggestion is that is comes from the London area of Chelsea, which, from the mid-nineteenth century, was favoured by artists who may have worn this seemingly more bohemian type of footwear. The Teddy boys of the 1950s revived the style – having no laces eliminated any interference at the top of the boot with the narrow cut of the trousers that were fashionable at the time – and it remains in vogue today.

RIGHT: Men's leather Chelsea, or elastic-sided, boots. These are early examples from 1880–1900, but the elastic gusset sides were replaced around 1962, when Chelsea boots became popular again.

ABOVE: A page from the catalogue *Footwear of Supreme Quality* representing Tanners Shoe Manufacturing Company, 493 C Street, Boston, Massachusetts, United States, Spring and Summer 1927. It highlights the choice for women with stout ankles!

OPPOSITE: These men's gold leather Balmoral boots would certainly cut a dash. Made by The Mounts Factory Co Ltd, Northampton, 1922.

THE FIRST WORLD WAR

The First World War had a tremendous impact on the shoe industry across the globe. In Europe, skilled men went off to fight, never to return. Those who did come back found their view of the world and their place in it much changed. Factory owners lost their heirs and struggled to survive post-war.

NEW ROLES FOR WOMEN

Across Europe, women took factory places vacated by men volunteering to fight. A new-found freedom influenced attitudes towards dress and culminated in a practical necessity for hard-wearing, functional shoes. Women driving ambulances, tending to the sick or undertaking other war work needed the right footwear. And, while fashion magazines emphasized a need for women to wear elegant shoes for their morale, extravagance and showy fashions were widely considered unpatriotic and not in keeping with the national tone.

THE BRITISH BOOT

Since the late 1880s the United States had dominated the shoe market, flooding Europe with mass-produced shoes (see pp. 110–11). Europe strove to catch up and, using technical innovations hailing from the United States, were well on their way to increasing factory output significantly. By 1913 The Economist news magazine published an article declaring 'Victory for the British Boot'. The declaration of war in the following year sealed that victory. In order to meet the demands of the war, boots and shoes were produced on an unprecedented scale, almost killing bespoke bootmaking. Seventy million pairs of boots were produced in Britain alone, with just fewer than fifty million being manufactured in Northamptonshire.

STURDY SHOES

Footwear for women during this time included styles that were sturdy, low-heeled and available in black or brown. With so many women experiencing bereavements, black was prevalent. The button or lace boot remained the most practical option until the 1920s. By that time it had also become acceptable for women to wear lace-up shoes. Leather and suede were common in winter and in summer there were options of white suede or buckskin, and beige or pale brown suede. While avoiding the restrictions that characterized the Second World War (see pp. 178–9),

there was nevertheless a move towards a pared-down economy in dress. A shortage of leather at the end of the war led to a rise in cloth-topped shoes and there were ideas in some of the fashion papers for transforming old and tired shoes using home-made bows and decorations.

ABOVE: Five women drivers of the First Aid Nursing Yeomanry (FANY) wearing fur coats while serving on the Western Front during World War One, c. 1916.

BELOW: Women's glacé, kid leather brogue Oxford shoes, 1914–19. Their sock is stamped 'W A Foster'.

RIGHT: Women's tan, glacé, kid leather lace boots, c. 1915. The trade name was Sorosis of A E Little & Co, Lynn, Massachusetts, United States. Sorosis shoe stores were located across the United States, and they also had stores in London and Manchester in England, Glasgow in Scotland, Berlin in Germany and Paris in France.

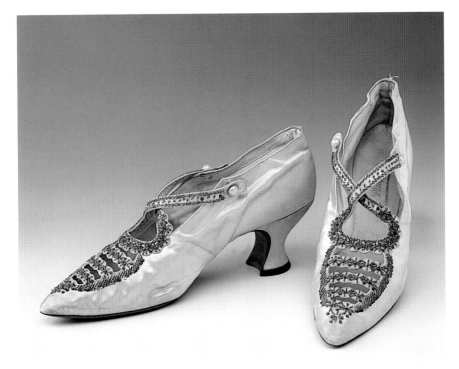

LEFT: Women's satin crossover evening shoes with a barrette vamp. Made by Dickins & Jones, 1901–10, they are decorated with sequins and beads. This looser shoe style would give greater flexibility when dancing.

THE UBIQUITOUS BAR SHOE

Europe entered an inevitable slump at the end of the First World War. Vital skilled workers had been lost and the economy was in recession. Things were about to change, however, with the introduction of a new and daring fashion that took Europe and the United States by storm.

Changes in attitude towards women's dress had been simmering since the turn of the twentieth century, when women began to rebel against the restrictive and formal clothing of the 1800s. From the 1920s onwards, hemlines grew significantly shorter and, by 1927, they were above the knee. This rise in hemline increased emphasis on the foot and attention turned to the shoe. This was the cue for some of the most beautiful shoes of the twentieth century. Simple yet effective styles emerged in a myriad of colours, materials and decorations. The shoemaking industry found itself expanding once more to meet demand.

PREVAILING STYLES

By 1924 the most popular style of women's shoe was the bar shoe, a simple design that involved a strap across the instep fastened with a single button. Various versions existed and included styles for daywear, sportswear and eveningwear. The shapely Louis heel (see pp. 142–43) was common and, a little later, a more slender version known by 1931 as the Spanish heel was added.

As hemlines continued to rise, other shoe styles emerged, including a bar shoe with multiple straps and a T-bar shoe, usually fastened with a buckle. There were also lace bar shoes, a Cromwell-style shoe with an extended tab, Oxfords, brogues and ghillies (the traditional Scottish style).

LEFT: A woman dressed for an evening out wearing a short slimline frock and a pair of satin bar shoes, 1920s.

BELOW: A woman's beaded and sequinned satin bar shoe, c. 1925. The sole is stamped 'Made in France', although the shoe was sold through Harrods of Knightsbridge, London, England.

LEFT: Women's gold, kid leather bar shoes with buckle decoration, 1924. The discovery of Egyptian King Tutankhamen's tomb in 1922 captivated designers throughout the Western world. Egyptian-inspired motifs found their way into designs for everything from crockery to clothing, and there was a passion for shimmering gold and turquoise coloured shoes.

ART-DECO STYLE

The art deco movement pioneered at the International Arts Exposition in Paris in 1925 found expression in shoes, which betrayed the influence of geometric shapes, strong lines and contrasting colours. Egyptian motifs found their way onto clothing and, of course, inspired shoes. Brightly coloured leathers and textiles were used to reflect the dazzling discovery. Dances including the Charleston and Black Bottom epitomized the Jazz era – and what better footwear is there for these rhythms than the closed-toe bar shoe with a low heel? Practical yet stylish, when made from silver and gold kid leather and adorned with diamanté accessories, it became the perfect shoe for the dance floor.

L'Ecureuil

LEFT: A fashion plate from 1922, entitled *'L'Ecureuil'* (The Squirrel), and advertising antelope and squirrel coats, *La Gazette de Bon Ton Année.*

155

HEELS AND TOES

As hemlines rose during the 1920s, the emphasis was clearly on shoes – and this extended to the heels and toes. New shapes began to emerge and, although heel innovations were largely associated with women's shoes, developments in toe design applied to both men's and women's footwear.

HEEL INNOVATIONS

In women's shoes, new heels were all the rage during this time. The Cuban heel, with a fairly straight side had been introduced in 1902. By the mid-twenties the heel had reached 4.5 cm (2 in) in height.

Carved wooden heels were covered with leather, fabric, paint or celluloid. A vertical slot was cut into the heel breast to receive the ends of the specific cover and then given a neat finish. Celluloid was often used for its smooth properties. It was softened first, by dipping it in acetone. Once placed around the heel, it shrank as it dried, resulting in a very tight-fitting cover. Leather layers could be printed onto the celluloid to give the idea of a stacked heel and this saved on finishing the heel, as all it needed was a polish. Sometimes diamanté and imitation jewels were set into the celluloid for a sparkling finish.

THE BULLDOG TOE

A new toe shape arrived in Europe in 1910, having originated in the United States. Known as the bulldog or Boston toe, the design raised the toe like a bump at the end of the shoe. It gave rise to a short stumpy look that was superseded in the 1920s by a more feminine, pointed toe.

MATERIALS OF CHOICE

New materials in use during the first quarter of the twentieth century included glacé leather, which went out of fashion in 1924 only to return a year later. Made from the skin of a young goat, glacé leather is chrome-tanned to produce a very glossy surface finish. Suede shoes – once all the rage – became impossible to sell by 1925 because the adhesive used in the lining gave it the reputation of 'drawing' the foot. Exotic leathers increased in popularity, with day and eveningwear styles available in snake, lizard and crocodile skin – all three, no doubt, sold with matching handbags.

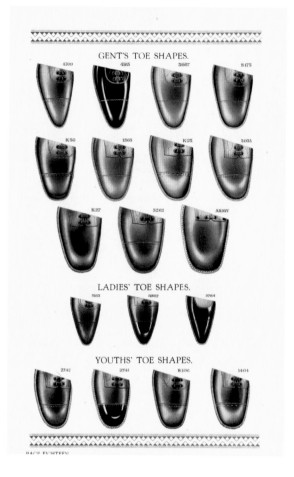

GENT'S TOE SHAPES.

LADIES' TOE SHAPES.

YOUTHS' TOE SHAPES.

LEFT: This page of toecap styles comes from the catalogue of Fred Knight Ltd, Rushden, Northamptonshire, c. 1925.

BELOW: The bulldog toe as seen in the catalogue of The Mounts Factory Co, Northampton, 1915.

BELOW: A bevy of jewelled heels, 1920s. The centre shoe was worn by the famous French music hall artist and showgirl, Mistinguett. She was the darling hit of Paris in the 1920s. Famous for her legs, it was rumoured she had insured them for one million pounds. She loved shoes and collected many high pairs in order to show off her assets.

THE CLASSIC BROGUE

Emerging in the 1890s and incredibly fashionable by 1905, the classic men's brogue had its origins in a style that was centuries old. *Brogue* is Gaelic for shoe and the birthplace of the brogue can be traced back to the simple, prehistoric footwear made in parts of Ireland – and in particular, on the Scottish Isle of Arran.

This early style began as a simple rectangle of cattle rawhide that was folded and seamed on each side using tarred string. The ends continued halfway up and were pulled together to form laces that tied. The resulting 'bag' was then moulded to the foot and worn with the hair on the outside to provide good grip. There are some wonderful examples of these early shoes on display in the National Museum of Ireland.

The Scottish uprising of 1745 did much to eliminate the influence of Scotland beyond its border for the best part of a century, and this style of shoe was all but forgotten in England. It was not until King George IV visited Scotland in 1822 that all things Scottish were promoted and celebrated -- including Scottish shoes.

PUNCHED HOLES AND WING CAPS

The punched holes that typify the design of the modern brogue developed from holes that were made in original incarnations of the shoe, in order to allow water to drain out when travelling through boggy territory. There is some evidence to suggest that this now decorative punching might also derive from the embellishments of late Elizabethan and early seventeenth-century footwear. At that time, it was fashionable to decorate shoes with fine cutwork, with pinked edges in geometric designs and stylized floral motifs. In later centuries, technological advances enabled such perforation and punching to become more uniform. It could be applied more easily and was used widely on the toecaps of both men's and women's shoes.

The brogue style embraced from the 1890s onwards usually sported a punched wing cap and counter seams. The wing cap describes the shape of the toecap, where a wing style has a peak at the centre line. The counter is the outside reinforcement on the quarters (those parts of the upper that join the vamp at the front of the shoe and each other at the back of the heel).

These wing caps became very fashionable and were frequently worn by royalty and golfers. The Prince of Wales was known for wearing a brogue with a fringed tongue. Black was the most popular colour initially, overtaken by

brown in the 1930s, once attitudes towards this 'informal' colour had relaxed somewhat. The 1920s and 1930s also saw a two-tone version, called the co-respondent, in combinations that included black and white or brown and cream (see pp. 174–5). The classic brogue style also became a popular footwear choice for women.

SHOES by *George Webb*

GEORGE WEBB & SONS (Northampton) LTD.
MAKERS OF FOOTWEAR FOR MEN
BROCKTON STREET
NORTHAMPTON   ENGLAND

LEFT: The brogue styles of George Webb & Sons, Brockton Street, Northampton, 1948, as seen in the volume *Presenting British Shoes and Leather*, published by the *Shoe and Leather News*. It highlighted the manufacturing of British companies after the Second World War.

OPPOSITE: The style inspired many different stylised versions, including this stunning black leather Oxford shoe (technically not a brogue), which is decorated with gold leather trim. Made by W L Douglas, 1930.

BELOW: Men's leather brogue Oxfords, 1930s. They were manufactured by George York & Sons, Long Buckby, Northamptonshire.

8

AUSTERITY YEARS

1930 to 1947

FROM BOOM TO BUST

The United States rapidly became the world's wealthiest nation in the years immediately following the First World War. Quicker to recover from the economic effects of warfare than Europe, US manufacturing shifted up a gear as the country entered a new phase of consumerism boosted by the spirit of what became dubbed the Roaring Twenties. Mass production of the automobile coincided with a cultural explosion – particularly in cities – which saw film, music and sport take centre stage, and women gained the right to vote. As European nations caught up they, too, embarked on a golden age.

The good times were short-lived, however, and came to an abrupt end with the Wall Street Crash of 1929. The United States was thrown into the Great Depression, the effects of which rippled throughout the world. High unemployment, widespread shortages and reduced wages signalled the end of the extravagant lifestyles of the previous decade. The 1930s heralded a more sober time that culminated in the start of the Second World War.

An understated elegance epitomized this era. It was certainly not as dramatic as the 1920s, but sophisticated nonetheless. Women's fashions were more tailored, the silhouette lengthened and greater importance was placed on the cut and fit of clothes. Such a look required a simple, elegant shoe and footwear fashions reflected this. The classic 1920s bar shoe, although still seen, waned in popularity while the T-bar and court shoe emerged as clear favourites.

LEADING INFLUENCES

European fashions, particularly those from Paris, faced the challenge of a new influence from the United States – that of the Hollywood film industry, which was hugely popular in the 1930s and 1940s. The emerging film stars of Tinseltown oozed a sophisticated glamour that people were desperate to emulate, particularly at a time when life was hard. Who could resist the charms of such screen sirens as Jean Harlow, Carole Lombard, Bette Davis and Joan Crawford?

There was also an increase in outdoor pursuits and activities during this era. The well-to-do were taking holidays and the suntan became a symbol of health and wealth. Coco Chanel helped make tans acceptable when pale skin had long been a symbol of the aristocracy and a life of indoor pastimes. Emphasis on the outdoors meant a need for suitable footwear, which in turn meant the rise of the sandal. American shoe companies dominated the ready-made market; Delman, I Miller and Palter employed freelance designers and exported their shoes all over the world.

WARTIME SHORTAGES

International communications became strained during the Second World War, and this resulted in a hiatus in the usual volley of fashion ideas between nations. In France, leather supplies became so scarce that manufacturers found it increasingly difficult to fulfil their own footwear orders, let alone any from abroad. In Britain, couture fashion designers such as Hardy Amies, Norman Hartnell and Victor Steibel became involved in creating a range of Utility designs for mass production.

Wartime austerity brought changes to women's shoe styles across Europe. The ability to express one's self fully through fashion was simply not an option, although it didn't stop women from trying with ingenious ways of making do and mending their shoes and customizing what they already owned.

Men's footwear in Europe changed little during the period. A palette of black and brown saw the Derby and Oxford styles dominate, with brogues and two-tone shoes added to the mix. Post-war there were five styles of demobilization 'demob' shoes in the UK – two Oxfords, two Derbys and a pair in brown suede.

1930S GLAMOUR

Although times were hard for many, there was always fashion to fall back on when morale was low. Boundaries between the types of shoe worn with specific outfits or at certain times of day had become blurred with the 'anything goes' attitude of the 1920s. This spontaneous freedom gave way to a more rigid etiquette in the 1930s.

Clothing became more refined during this period, with designated outfits for specific times of day and for specific pastimes. A wide selection of shoes for daywear, eveningwear, work, sporting activities, town and country reflected this (see quote).

PREVAILING STYLES

Women, now wearing trousers for casual wear, required an appropriate shoe style for their new elongated silhouettes. The 1920s bar shoe, though popular, gave way to its rival, the T-bar shoe, which became available in softer colours. It was more streamlined, too, and had a higher, more elegant heel approaching 7.5 cm (3 in) in some models. Pastels were popular from the mid-1930s, as were a range of jewel colours and metallic leathers. Black was the colour of choice for eveningwear, trimmed with gold or silver.

In comparison with the closed-bar shoe, there was a marked increase in exposing more of the foot. Slingback sandals and peep toes were becoming widely worn. At the end of the 1930s this elegance gave way to wedge heels, cork soles and the rather chunky platform (see pp. 170–1).

ABOVE: Five elegant women walking in fur coats and wearing a variety of shoe styles from the 1930s.

RIGHT: An advertisement for Dolcis shoes including a selection of high-heeled, peep-toe sandals in various colours, June 1937.

OPPOSITE: A pair of women's black and gold evening ankle strap sandals decorated with green and orange floral embroidery, 1933.

'To have shoes on one's feet is now more nearly described as to be wearing the kind of shoes dictated by time of day and circumstances. The nuances between active sports shoes, walking shoes, stroll in the park shoes and smart afternoon shoes are clearly visible.'

French Vogue, 1936.

SANDALS

The sandal was very popular throughout the 1930s for beach and summer wear and sporty leisure activities. Not seen on women's feet for hundreds of years, the sandal slowly permeated all aspects of life to find itself worn on the dance floor and, in a modified form, as smart daywear. Open-toed versions emerged from the mid-1930s and slingback styles soon followed.

Despite the shoe's popularity, *Vogue* magazine expressed shock at such a vulgar display of exposed foot and casualness and declared the sandal unhygienic and bad for the feet. The style was deemed to be the choice of a woman who showed a distinct lack of good taste. It was also thought that such shoes should only be worn for eveningwear, as the exposed toe was akin to going naked during the day!

During the Second World War, shortages in certain materials meant that designers had to seek alternatives. The Italian designer Elsa Schiaparelli took inspiration from woven baskets in local markets and fashioned multicoloured woven uppers for a range of sandals.

ROPE-WOVEN SOLES

The espadrille had been made in Spain for hundreds of years. Its name derived from esparto – the grass used for making the rope soles. The style became popular as leisure- and beachwear among the moneyed and well-travelled classes during the 1920s and 1930s, when they could be seen on the beaches of the Côte d'Azur. A unisex shoe, it came in various tailored styles. John F Kennedy posed in a pair on holiday with his sisters for *American Vogue* in 1938. Salvador Dalí was also spotted wearing them, though they were certainly not mainstream men's fashion at this time.

ABOVE: A fashion plate from *La Chaussure*, 1939. It shows a selection of sandals available, including a knitted option (shown bottom).

ESPADRILLES

Espadrilles made from woven esparto grass and cotton have been made in Catalan, Spain, since the thirteenth century and were originally worn by peasants who could not afford leather shoes. People around the world quickly adopted the style because it was made from materials that were cheap and easy to obtain. This pair dates from c. 1900.

BELOW: This pair of women's grey tweed morning or beach clogs was made by R R Bunting of London and Paris, 1936. They have 10 cm (4 in) wooden heels with wooden platform soles. A leather insole acts as a hinge to the segmented wooden sole.

SALVATORE FERRAGAMO

An extremely influential figure from this period was Salvatore Ferragamo, renowned for his use of diverse materials. Born in 1898, Ferragamo was quick to realize that the American shoe industry was far ahead of Europe at the turn of the twentieth century and he crossed the Atlantic in 1914 to learn the ready-made trade.

SHOEMAKER TO THE STARS

After working for the Quality Queen factory in New York, Ferragamo realized that his passion for making quality, crafted footwear could not be satisfied by factory manufacturing. Inspired by the burgeoning Hollywood scene, he moved to the West Coast in 1923 and set up a workshop making bespoke footwear for the glamorous film stars of the day. His clients included Gloria Swanson, Clara Bow, Mary Pickford and Rudolph Valentino. Hollywood success and, therefore, demand for his shoes, finally outstripped production and in 1927 he returned to Italy.

TIRELESS IMPROVISATION

Ferragamo produced innovative originals that demonstrated his inexhaustible imagination. He popularized the wedge heel, from 1936, and the platform. Wedge heels had featured as sports footwear during the 1920s, but Ferragamo brought the style up to date with a very modern and daring twist. He also popularized the cork sole and spool heel – in which the heel had a waist, rather like a cotton reel. He is, perhaps, best known for his amazing sculptured platform-soled sandals, which echoed the fashion of the day and reached new, breathtakingly glamorous heights.

In 1935 the League of Nations imposed sanctions and restrictions on Italy to try and stop their continued aggression towards Ethiopia. Challenged by this, Ferragamo was unable to make traditional leather footwear, so he began to improvise with those materials that were available to him – cellophane, raffia, string and fish skin.

When he could no longer obtain steel, he developed the Sardinian cork wedge. Receiving a lukewarm reception at first, it went on to be one of the most popular styles of the war years. It was fashionable, yet comfortable and easy to wear. And, making good use of alternative materials, they were perfect for the wartime economy. In 1939 Ferragamo estimated that 86 per cent of all American women's shoes were made with a wedge heel!

1950S GLAMOUR

The sophisticated and glamorous Italian film industry, the rise in tourism and a greater awareness of Italian style made Italy the place to be and be seen. Movie stars and personalities flocked to Italy, making a beeline for Ferragamo to pick up a pair of shoes oozing with Italian style. The Italians were a force to be reckoned with during this time. No longer imitating the French leading designers, they produced their own styles and looks. Marilyn Monroe was a Ferragamo fan and is wearing a pair of his shoes as her dress blows up as she stands over the air vent in *The Seven Year Itch*!

LEFT: Salvatore Ferragamo guides a woman into a pair of shoes, 1950.

OPPOSITE: This elegantly sculptured, wedge-heeled shoe was designed and made by Salvatore Ferragamo, 1948–50. The curved, undercut heel provides the shoe with a striking focal point. Both style and colour echo the earlier chopine and the richness of the Italian Renaissance.

THE PLATFORM SOLE

While the elegant, streamlined T-bar shoe had characterized the start of the 1930s, by the end of the decade, the platform sole was centre stage, with its clumpy and chunky look. First finding popularity as beachwear, the style subsequently entered mainstream fashion.

The platform existed in both a high-end version – by such designers as Ferragamo, Vivier and Perugia, who managed to transform it into something quite spectacular – to those available on the high street. The most spectacular, and certainly iconic, pair were those that Ferragamo designed for the Hollywood star Judy Garland in 1938. They have a gold, kid leather ankle strap and strappy vamp, coupled with a cork platform covered in jewel-coloured suede to create an undulating look.

When Vivier – the first proponent of the style – sent his original platform-soled design to his manufacturer Herman B Delman in the mid-1930s, Delman's response was, 'Are you crazy?' The last time platforms had been seen was on the towering chopine (see pp. 30–1) so, to many, this style was rather more reminiscent of the practical orthopaedic shoe (see quote). It is said that Vivier took his inspiration from a small pair of Chinese platform slippers he found in Paris. Reception to the style was lukewarm at first but, once Delman began to manufacture thousands of pairs and customers included such fashion luminaries as Marlene Dietrich and Marilyn Monroe, the style appeared in his chain stores across the United States.

A 1930s star forever associated with platform-soled sandals was Brazilian actress Carmen Miranda, who combined towering turban headdresses decorated with fruit with equally towering platforms, to become the 'Brazilian Bombshell'. Many of her wonderfully over the top platforms were designed by Ted Savel of California.

'Whereas French women only wear orthopaedic sandals in the house or on the beach, Italian women have literally gone mad about the wedge.'

Harper's Bazaar, July 1938.

ABOVE: A pair of women's silver brocade and kid leather court shoes, made by Lotus Ltd, Northampton, 1946.

ABOVE: Woman's leather platform-sole court shoe, made by Denson, United States, 1946.

MEN'S FOOTWEAR

Changes in men's footwear were less dramatic during this period than those seen in women's fashions. Although boots remained popular, certain styles had fallen by the wayside, including the Chelsea boot by 1920 (see pp. 150–1) and the button boot by 1930. The front-laced boot was still the most popular practical boot, but it was certainly not stylish enough for smart day- or eveningwear.

Oxford and Derby shoes (see pp. 122–3) dominated as the style of choice – usually in black and, eventually, brown – with a low, leather, stacked heel. The more adventurous one's choice of colour, the more fashionable one was perceived to be, and the two-tone, or co-respondent shoe as it was known by 1941 (see pp. 174–5), was the most obvious 'dandy' of choices. In fact, it was a practical shoe for these austerity years, since combining colours in this way diverted attention from any imperfections in the leather.

THE MONK SHOE

A new style that appeared during this time was the Monk shoe, a plain-fronted, low-cut, slip-on style that had a high tongue with a wide strap across the instep which attached to a buckle. Said to have originated in styles worn by fifteenth-century Alpine monks, this modern interpretation was first seen in the United Kingdom in 1927. Other European countries subsequently adopted the style. The monk was considered less formal than an Oxford shoe, but more formal than the Derby.

A Kendall advert declared: 'A monk shoe – the new craze'. By 1935, Northampton firm John Marlow and Sons and the Army and Navy Store were advertising the style for women, too, with 'buckles, brown or box calf at 30/- a pair'. By now the style sported narrower straps. In 1942 the Monk style became one of the first to be manufactured with a wooden sole.

THE APRON FRONT

The apron front (a boot or shoe with an oval-ended apron stitched to the top of the vamp) was introduced and seen on styles that were referred to as the Norwegian or Ski style. Essentially, the design was based on a moccasin.

The apron front appeared when men's clothing became more casual – around 1936 in the United Kingdom. It became a popular style in America, where it could be found in black, brown and tan leather.

Model 3027   Brown Calf Brogue. ⁵⁄₁₆" leather sole.

Model 3044   Brown Calf Gibson with front of interweave calf for coolness. ¼" leather sole.

Model 3031   Brown Calf and White Buckskin Brogue Monk. ⅜" crepe sole. Can also be supplied with Biege Elk or leather soles.

Model 3030   Brown Suede Monk Shoe in light, medium or dark brown. ⁵⁄₁₆" leather sole.

Model 3092   Golden Calf Ski Gibson. Storm welt and ⅜" waterproof leather sole. Can also be supplied with sports rubber soles.

Model 2969   Brown Calf Semi Brogue Oxford, ⁵⁄₁₆" leather sole.

Exeldia SHOES

Made by

EATON & CO. (RUSHDEN) LTD.
Rushden   •   Northants

Men's 31

ABOVE: This page featured in the volume *Presenting British Shoes and Leather*, published by the *Shoe and Leather News* in 1948. It highlights styles for men made by Eaton & Co (Rushden) Ltd, Northamptonshire.

THE CO-RESPONDENT

This classic two-tone shoe – essentially an Oxford or Derby style (see pp. 122–3) with a contrasting toecap, counter and facings – reached its peak of popularity in Europe and the United States in the 1930s, though the style had been around for some time by then.

A white shoe with contrasting black or brown leather piecework had been popular as sportswear since the 1860s. In England, the *Boot and Shoemaker* journal of June 1878 shows an image of such a boot made for cricket by a Mr Lobb. It illustrates a white boot with smooth dark leather counters (an outside reinforcement on the quarters), tarsal strap, toecap and facings (the front part of the quarters carrying the eyelets or lace holes). It is thought that they were originally designed this way because these areas took most of the wear during sporting activities.

NAMING THE SHOE

The style became fashionable as daywear during the 1920s Jazz Age in the United States. Some say the English name for the style, the 'co-respondent', was inspired by the dubious characters that would, for instance, be co-respondents in a divorce case. Other sources claim that the name stemmed from a conversation between Lacy Alexander of Lotus Shoe Company, Northampton, England, and a Mr Thomson of the Professional Golfers' Association, in which they used the term 'co-respondent' to describe the famous 'Lotus Dormy One' golf shoe (which had this two-tone style). Either way, the name stuck. In America the style is known as the spectator shoe, since it was the footwear of choice among spectators at sporting and other events.

THE TWO-TONE LOOK

Certainly the 1920s and 1930s were the high point for the co-respondent style. It was extremely fashionable among the wealthy on holiday around the Côte d'Azur and popular for

LEFT: A man cutting a dash in co-respondent/spectator wing-tip brogues with silk socks and striped trousers, 1940s.

weekend wear. The style came in many different colours, of which the three most popular were black and white, brown and white, and beige and brown. Famous wearers included the Hollywood dancer Fred Astaire, who wore a lighter version to dance in. The Duke of Windsor was often seen wearing two-tone shoes, and in fact wore tan and white co-respondents during a 1925 visit to the United States, further popularizing them as golf shoes in 1937.

The two-tone look was also popular with women, particularly in the 1930s. Mrs Churchill wore them, as did the film star Jean Harlow, whose pair was decorated with mock appliqué.

RIGHT: Men's hand-sewn brown and white leather brogue Oxford shoes in the co-respondent or spectator style, 1930–4. They sport the classic wingtip toecap.

SHOES FOR ATHLETES
THE OLYMPIC GAMES, BERLIN 1936

An increased interest in sports and outdoor activities was further endorsed during this period by the 1936 Olympics, which not only saw the American athlete Jesse Owens win four gold medals, defiant in the face of Adolf Hitler, but also spotlighted the sports footwear manufactured by the Dazzler brothers (Adolf 'Adi' and Rudolph), who went on to form two of the biggest sportswear companies of the twentieth and twenty-first centuries.

Adi Dassler began making handmade sports footwear in 1923. He persuaded his brother Rudolph to join him and, on 1 July 1924, the Gebrüder Dassler Schuhfabrik (Dassler Brothers' Shoe Company) was registered in their hometown of Herzogenaurach, Germany. By 1927 the firm was producing one hundred pairs of shoes a day.

Dassler developed specialized shoes with cleats (metal spikes) for sprinting and middle-distance running up to eight hundred metres. The shoes had goatskin uppers, insoles made of chrome splits and a sole made from vegetable-tanned leather. They were designed to be lightweight and to fit the foot like a glove, enhancing performance.

Athletes wore these specialized spiked track shoes for the first time in the 1928 Olympic Games in Amsterdam. Seemingly unaffected by the Depression of the 1930s, the company forged ahead. During the 1932 Olympics in Los Angeles, German athlete Arthur Jonath won bronze in the one-hundred-metre sprint wearing Dassler shoes.

The Dasslers' finest moment came at the Berlin Olympics in 1936. When Jessie Owens won his gold medals, he was wearing their shoes for all four events. Success led to product expansion and, by 1938, the company was making thirty different sports shoes for eleven sporting events including football boots, tennis shoes and ice skates.

THE BIRTH OF ADIDAS
After years of working together the Dassler brothers had an irreconcilable row and went their separate ways. Rudolph went on to establish Puma in 1948 and, in August 1949, Adi registered adidas (a combination of his nickname and last name). The official company name was 'Adolf Dassler adidas Sportschuhfabrik'. First used in 1949, the company's iconic three stripes remain one of world's most famous sporting symbols and the key identifier of the adidas brand.

ABOVE: Jesse Owens, four times champion at the Olympic Games in Berlin, Germany, August 1936.

BELOW: Adidas running shoes made from goatskin. They were worn by Sir Christopher Chattaway when he completed a 4 minute mile at the White City Stadium, London in 1955.

BELOW: Men's dark red and cream leather Puma Tip training shoes, made in the former West Germany, 1950–9. The shoe features the company's early logo of the cat jumping through the Dassler D, so they were made well before the famous stripe logo was introduced. They are among the oldest surviving Puma training shoes and incredibly rare.

WARTIME LIMITATIONS

The start of the Second World War signalled great change for the shoe industry. Early on it was clear that huge efforts would be required to equip the armed forces (see pp. 184–5). It was also apparent that the war would affect the civilian population on a much greater level than had been seen during the First World War (see pp. 152–3).

Such was the scale of hardship that governments across Europe and the United States introduced rationing and utility schemes. Civilians, though not entirely happy with the idea of such restrictions, were more fed up with finding themselves at the receiving end of unfair distribution and profiteering – but they put up little resistance.

RATIONING STAMPS AND COUPONS

Introduced in Germany in 1939, France in 1940 and the United Kingdom in 1941, rationing was perceived as fair to all in such difficult times. All three systems involved the use of stamps that could be exchanged in return for food, clothing and shoes. Rationing Tables were published detailing the number of coupons required for certain items. For example, in England, a man needed seven coupons for a pair of boots or shoes, while a boy's pair required three. A pair of adult leggings, gaiters or spats could be had for three coupons – two for a boy's pair. Slippers, boots or shoes for an adult woman required five coupons per pair, whereas three were required for a girl. Initially the coupon allowance was sixty-six coupons per person per year, but in 1942 this figure dropped to forty-eight.

RESTRICTIONS IN THE UNITED STATES

Wartime rationing was not just limited to European countries. From 1943 in the United States each person was rationed to three pairs of shoes a year and the shoes were only available in six standard-issue colours. Heel height in women's shoes was limited to 2.5 cm (1 in), whereas in the United Kingdom heels were deemed acceptable at 5 cm (2 in) before they came under strict scrutiny.

THE UTILITY STANDARD

In the United Kingdom, the Utility scheme had to comply with the government's 'Making up of Civilian Clothing (Restriction)' orders, which limited and monitored the types of materials used and fixed the prices.

Quality was controlled by the Limitations of Supplies Order, where companies had to supply 50 per cent of their footwear to Utility standards and in the case of children's footwear, 75 per cent. In order to distinguish such footwear, and indeed clothing, such items were stamped with the Utility mark. There were many complaints about the Utility standard.

The Utility order set out to monitor quality and would, reported Christopher Sladen, 'ensure economical usage of material and labour without detracting from appearance.' Utility designs were produced by designers of the day, including Hardy Amies, Victor Stiebel and Norman Hartnell for mass production.

BELOW: A pair of women's leather and water python snakeskin court shoes, 1942. They are stamped on the lining with the Utility mark.

RIGHT: A page from the catalogue of Frederick Riley Ltd, Gainsborough Shoe Works, Stafford, England, showing a range of women's styles available in 1948.

" Gainsborough " model in white grain calf, casual. Elastic fitting. Welted crepe sole and crepe heel.

" Gainsborough " model in black suede and black calf " Orchid " trimmed court shoe. Delmac flexible process, 2¼ in. covered Louis heel.

" Gainsborough " model in lilac blue calf, peep-toe court shoe. Delmac flexible process. 2¼ in. covered heel.

"Gainsborough" model in "Tutsan" calf, three-eyelet tie shoe. Delmac flexible process. 2 in. covered Cuban heel.

GAINSBOROUGH
SHOES

Made by
FREDERICK RILEY LTD.
GAINSBOROUGH SHOE WORKS
STAFFORD • ENGLAND

MAKE DO AND MEND

With the restrictions that came with the Second World War, it was not long before civilians, and women in particular, became adept at making do and mending – in many cases modifying – items of clothing that they already had in their wardrobes. This, of course, extended to footwear. The simple addition of some embroidery threads, along with costume jewellery and dyes, did much to revitalize faded footwear.

POSTER CAMPAIGNS

In the United Kingdom, the government created Mrs Sew and Sew, a resourceful and handy seamstress who encouraged such ingenious and inventive behaviour. Women honed their dressmaking skills to make 'new' items of clothing out of old: a coat from an old bedspread, a child's outfit from a pair of trousers. Buttons, zips and other accessories were saved and reused. Creativity was the key, although it must have been incredibly hard for those with little or no dressmaking skill or flair.

Many handy hint leaflets gave advice on how to take care of clothing, utilize patches and get the best wear from your shoes. Shoe polish wasn't available so people were advised to cut a potato in half and use the tuber to bring a shine to their boots and shoes.

Stockings were scarce and women frequently knitted ankle socks, reusing wool from jumpers. And it was not unusual to paint bare legs with gravy browning and run a line of pencil down the back of the leg to represent a seam. One just prayed that it didn't rain!

RIGHT: Created during the war, this *Make Do and Mend* poster offered serious advice that had to be adhered to in times of austerity, 1940s.

BELOW: Women's leather, wedge-heeled, bar-strap shoes, 1947. They have a mock toecap with punched decoration to echo the detail of a brogue. Practical, they are nevertheless cheery in their red leather.

MONEY-SAVING MATERIALS

Wartime rationing may give the overriding impression that all women's footwear was dull and boring during the war years, but that was not the case. Alongside the thousands of practical workaday styles, a number of innovative designs emerged using a wide range of materials.

The wedge heel introduced by Salvatore Ferragamo in 1936 (see pp. 168–9) remained fashionable for women during the war, albeit in lower models. With the bulk of good leather going to the manufacturers producing footwear for the armed forces (see pp. 184–5), fashion manufacturers had to be resourceful. They turned to a wide range of materials that may have raised an eyebrow or two had it not been for the war. It was not uncommon, for example, to see shoes made with heels or platforms using exotic skins, transforming otherwise poor-quality shoes into something quite stunning. Crocodile, lizard and snake were all used as an alternative to calf leather.

Natural resources came to the fore across Europe. In Norway and Denmark an abundance of fish gave rise to many pairs of fish-skin shoes with matching handbags! Plaice was a popular choice. Inferior leather was disguised using bright dyes and textured pebble surfaces. Perhaps surprisingly, brightly coloured shoes were very popular during this time, providing an all-important morale boost. Cheaper alternatives were also found for soles – including cork, wood and crêpe – while uppers were frequently made from canvas, plastic, felt and raffia.

CLOGS

To help with the shortages of and limitations on footwear during the war, wooden-soled shoes were introduced in 1943. Requiring a mere two coupons as opposed to five for women – by saving on thick sole leather – they were an attempt at 'eking out the nation's leather.'

Unfortunately their ration-book cheapness and practical support for the leather trades did not make them any more appealing to the wearer. In August 1944 *The Boot Trades Association Gazette* reported that 'the retailer has had great difficulty in persuading his customer to buy his [wooden soled] shoe (to relieve the demand for leather). After the novelty had fallen off, retailers began to experience difficulty in maintaining sales.'

BELOW LEFT: Women's blue and gold tanned fish-skin evening sandals, 1950. The shoes were sold with a matching drawstring handbag and were made in Denmark.

BELOW: Woman's snake and cork-soled slingback sandal, 1945–9. The sock is stamped 'Manguins of Paris, France'.

RIGHT: Women's lace-up shoes with openwork raffia uppers in red, green, blue, yellow and brown, 1947–9. The shoes have a crêpe rubber sole with the edge of the sole and heel covered in woven string. Made by Manfield & Sons, Northampton.

THE WAR EFFORT

For the duration of the Second World War, factories throughout Europe and in the United States were dedicated to manufacturing military footwear on a grand scale. Manufacturers found themselves producing boots and shoes on a massive scale and for a wide range of military situations.

The war was not just fought on land and at sea, but also in arctic and tropical conditions, beneath the sea and in the desert. Meanwhile, women were conscripted into roles that included non-combative jobs in the military. From 1941, in the United Kingdom footwear included shoes and boots for the WRENS (Women's Royal Naval Service) and ATS (Auxiliary Territorial Service), and in the United States from 1942, for the WAACS (Women's Army Corp) and WAAVES (Women Accepted for Volunteer Emergency Service). Princess Elizabeth joined the ATS in February 1945 at the age of nineteen and reached the rank of junior commander. Northampton Museum has a replica of the brown leather lace-up shoes made for her as a 2nd subaltern in the ATS by Dawn Shoes, Northampton.

VARIETY OF FOOTWEAR

There were requests for many styles of footwear, including an aircraft rigger's boot, the Marine Corp field shoe, a navy submarine sandal, an army nurse white lace-up shoe, a ski boot, a parachute jumper boot, the US Mukluk designed for extremely dry cold and worn over several pairs of socks, the Alaskan service boot and the jungle boot.

Shoe factories were instructed to meet the requirements laid down by their governments. Any shoe factory that could focus on war production did so, including Converse in the United States, who manufactured the Air Force flying boots, and the Dassler factory in Germany, making army boots. All footwear manufacturers – utility and military – had to follow strict rules and regulations. In 1944 the United States published a *Wartime Encyclopaedia of Terminology Regulations*, which highlighted that 'Almost every phase of operations of leather, shoes and leather products is covered by government regulations issued in an effort to supply the military, conserve critical materials and maintain a sane price structure.' For example the entry for Athletic Shoes reads: 'In Sept. 1944, non-leather shoes with rubber soles were classed as ration free.'

THE ESCAPE BOOT

One of the iconic styles to emerge from the United Kingdom during this time was the ingenious escape boot, a high-legged leather boot with a fleece layer over a shrapnel-proof lining consisting of loose layers of silk. The boot's unique feature was that the leg section could be cut away from the vamp using a knife that was concealed in a pocket inside one of the boots. The result was a normal-looking Derby shoe (see pp. 122–3). Should a pilot be forced to abandon his aircraft over enemy territory, his clothing might well pass muster but the boot would clearly mark him out. By turning the boot into a shoe, however, the pilot had less chance of being discovered.

RIGHT: The escape boot was designed by Ron Kitchin for Haynes and Cann, Northampton, England, 1943. This pair still has its penknife, tucked into a small pocket inside the boot.

9

A NEW ERA

1947 TO THE 1970s

MID-CENTURY OPTIMISM

The Second World War left widespread destruction on a monumental scale – major European cities lay in ruins; families had been separated for years, many of them displaced and without homes; and there were huge personal losses for victims of the Holocaust and soldiers who died in action. Despite the horror – and to a large extent because of it – countries recovering from the war did so with profound optimism. Many countries – the US, Germany, Italy, Britain, Japan – entered phases of unprecedented growth. Rapid modernization and urbanization gave rise to expanding middle classes and much improved standards of living. Consumerism was beginning to drive society in ways never seen before.

A RETURN TO FEMININITY

Initially women were encouraged to return home from their wartime endeavours and take up the more traditional role of wife, mother and homemaker. There was a push to leave wartime austerity behind, while aiming for a bit of glamour and beauty. Rationing in much of Europe continued into the 1950s, and although the sturdy and practical footwear of the Second World War took some time to be ousted, when a relaxation of the restrictions finally came, so too did a greater flare for fashion. For women, the peep toe, so frivolous at the start of the war, returned, as did higher heels and short snub toes.

Christian Dior's New Look of 1947 transformed the way women dressed in the 1950s. Naturally, Dior's New Look demanded an appropriate style of shoe. No longer desirable, the practical wedges and platforms of the 1930s and 1940s made way for a court shoe with a high slender heel that perfectly complemented Dior's overtly feminine look. This decade also saw better living conditions, increased prosperity and the advent of American rock and roll. It was around this time that the teenager was born.

THE LONDON LOOK

The 1960s heralded dramatic changes throughout the fashion world, with many of the prevalent styles remaining refreshingly modern to this day. At the beginning of the decade, Parisian designers were still dominant but the formal look faded and a more casual and sexy style took its place. As the 1960s progressed, London usurped Paris as the capital of the fashion world. Couture came under attack, with boutiques opening that catered to the tastes of the teenager. Older women tried to look like their daughters – young and slim with long legs. Many styles and fads characterize this period, from Mary Quant's miniskirts to André Courrège's space-age look, to musically influenced styles, such as those of the mod and the hippy. Experimentation with new materials was rife – there were paper dresses, PVC, plastics and Corfam.

FROM PLATFORMS TO PUNK

By the end of the 1960s, a certain disillusionment had sunk in and the beginning of the pick-me-up 1970s arrived in the form of platform-soled glam rockers. The craze for chunky, towering platforms was cut short by the global depression that followed the oil crisis of 1973, and a return to more conservative styles. During this decade a more casual and natural look, which manifested as blue jeans coupled with red leather Kickers, made its way to Europe from America. This new style of comfortable yet fashionable boots was created by French fashion visionary Daniel Raufest.

  By the late 1970s the UK scene was in the grip of a punk rebellion. With a complete disregard for conventional fashion and an emphasis on 'in-your-face' aggression and nonconformity, punks adopted an eclectic range of footwear from the high-heeled stiletto court and pointed-toed winklepicker to the practical Dr Martens boot.

THE NEW LOOK

As Great Britain continued to battle with wartime austerity towards the end of the 1940s, French couture was on the rise again, with Paris leading the way. One designer in particular was about to take the world by storm with his overtly feminine Corolle line of 1947. His name was Christian Dior.

Dubbed the New Look in the United States, Dior's style focused on a nipped-in waist, a full, flowing skirt and a high-heeled court shoe – forerunner of the stiletto (see pp. 192–3). All told, the style was the epitome of feminine elegance.

In Britain, politicians were quick to criticize the New Look and its excessive use of material, but they were swimming against the tide. Dior's creation was a stylish breath of fresh air, and after years of practical clothing, rationing and making do and mending, women on both sides of the Atlantic were keen to embrace it. The style screamed femininity, and this was exactly what was needed in the wake of the hard practicalities of war.

THE STEEL HEEL

Of course, high heels had existed in the past and, in order to bear the weight of the wearer, they had had to be thick – made from stacked leather or carved in wood and covered. Now Dior demanded shoes with extended and pointed toes but also a slender heel. How to achieve this? Initially shoemakers adapted the wooden heel by incorporating a moulded metal stem inside it. This gave sufficient support to enable a more slender heel. Although not technically a 'stiletto' heel, the metal ends of such footwear caused a certain amount of damage to wooden floors – a precursor of what was to come.

BELOW: These delightful, pink silk, ankle-tie evening shoes were designed by Roger Vivier in 1957. They demonstrate his skill and obvious delight in creating such feminine shoes.

LEFT: A pair of blue satin court shoes, *c.* 1955. Their pink satin sock is stamped in gold: 'Christian Dior, Harrods, London'. An incredibly elegant pair of shoes, it sports the recently invented stiletto heel.

THE STILETTO

The growth of the shoe industry that followed the Second World War was boosted by Christian Dior's New Look (see pp. 190–1). This era was characterized by increased vigour and ingenuity. There was a desire to move on and embrace the new post-war age with great optimism. In the midst of all this activity, the stiletto heel was born.

PARIS LEADS THE WAY

Once more, Paris became the centre of the fashion world, with shoe designer Roger Vivier (see pp. 194–5) taking credit for inventing the stiletto heel. As shoe designer to Christian Dior from 1953, Vivier designed bespoke shoes for Dior's couture collection as well as models for a ready-made series that carried both of their names on the label. The New Look was complemented perfectly by Vivier's high-heeled court shoes, and eventually the stiletto, but the claim to such a groundbreaking credit is not quite so clear-cut.

VIVIER'S TIMING

Vivier used cutting-edge injection-moulding techniques that allowed him to create a slender plastic heel of incredible strength – a heel that he called 'the needle'.

Some might say that Vivier was simply lucky that such advances in technology coincided with his time with Dior and that, in reality, manufacturers and designers had been striving to create such a heel for many years. As such, the invention of the stiletto heel has to be considered as a collaborative progression. In France André Perugia and Charles Jourdan were obsessed with designing a slender heel, as were Beth Levine and Herman Delman in the United States and, of course, Ferragamo in Italy. Almost able to taste success, they were pipped to the post by the combined publicity savvy of Dior's couture house and Vivier's sheer determination.

TAKING THE WORLD BY STORM

The stiletto's first mention in England appeared in *The Telegraph* newspaper on 10 September 1953. Soon after that, the style was adopted throughout Europe and the United States. In Italy, the heel reached new heights, quite literally, and attracted glamorous celebrities that included Marilyn Monroe. Often quoted is the journalist Jimmy Starr's comment that Marilyn 'learned the trick of cutting a quarter inch off one heel so that when she walked she would wiggle.' Her passion for Ferragamo stilettos saw her wear them in memorable films such as *Gentlemen Prefer Blondes*, *Bus Stop* and *The Seven Year Itch*.

'I don't know who invented the high heel, but women owe him a lot.'

Marilyn Monroe.

OPPOSITE: These cerise satin, stiletto-heeled court shoes were designed by Christian Dior, *c.* 1960. The outer edges are decorated with two satin bows with diamanté centres.

LEFT: A model poses in Paris, 1958. She wears the very latest in fashion – a pencil skirt and stiletto shoes.

THE STILETTO PARADOX

A high heel is a paradox: on the one hand the wearer is empowered, standing tall and majestic, overshadowing everyone. A woman in high heels rapidly becomes an object of male worship. Yet, on the other hand, a high heel tends to restrict movement, hindering a woman's escape from that obsessive worship.

ROGER VIVIER

Roger Vivier was a master couturier of the woman's foot. A heady combination of exquisite decoration, lightness of touch and the utmost precision reinforced his own belief that successful shoe construction depended on the harmony of form. This ability to make something so perfect made Vivier one of the most innovative and sought-after designers of the twentieth century.

From the 1930s onwards, Vivier began a long association with the American shoe manufacturer Herman B Delman. Although he opened his first shop on the fashionable rue Royale, Paris, in 1937, he was forced to flee for New York during the Second World War, where he continued to make shoes until wartime restrictions made it too difficult. Returning to Paris once the war was over, Vivier joined the house of Dior, creating one of the most successful collaborative partnerships in the history of fashion.

Aside from garnering credit for creating the stiletto heel (see pp. 192–3), Vivier is renowned for having introduced many diverse heel shapes, including the comma with its flared-out silhouette, the pyramid, the choc (a slender, curved stiletto heel), the escargot, the needle, the spool, the prism and the ball (in which a stiletto heel emerges from a rounded top of heel). It should come as no surprise that he was nicknamed the 'heel king'. Vivier was also one of the first designers to use clear plastic.

Following the death of Christain Dior in 1957, Vivier designed for Yves Saint Laurent. He also ghosted designs for Bally and Rayne in the 1950s. Prohibitively expensive and therefore not worn by many, Vivier's designs are beautifully decorated. Some say they were more beautiful than wearable. One famous client was Queen Elizabeth II of England, who wore a pair of gold kid leather shoes made by Vivier for her coronation in 1953.

BELOW: Women's psychedelic-patterned silk court shoes or pumps, designed by Roger Vivier in the late 1960s.

'My shoes are sculptures. They are quintessentially French, a Parisian alchemy of style.'

Roger Vivier.

BELOW: This blue silk court shoe with lavish beaded embellishment was created by Roger Vivier, the 'Fabergé of shoes' in 1961. It is a perfect example of Vivier's skill in combining innovative structure with dramatic ornamentation. The shoe is complete with Vivier's iconic comma heel, and echoes the exotic slippers of the Middle East.

THE CLASSIC COURT SHOE

The late 1940s onwards saw the dominance of what can only be described as the classic court shoe for women. First seen in the late nineteenth century (see pp. 116–17), this style of shoe now epitomized the new feminine look of the 1950s and the shape of things to come.

A leading proponent of the style in the United Kingdom was the distinguished H & M Rayne, whose first shoe shop opened on Bond Street, London, in 1920.

Rayne was quick to spot emerging trends and make the most of them. By the 1950s, he'd taken a keen interest in the new designs and technological innovations gaining ground in France and Italy. At the same time, he established licensing deals with distinguished department stores Bergdorf Goodman and Bonwit Teler in New York, giving his company a much-needed international boost. Rayne shoes were also associated with Delman.

RAYNE DESIGNS

Rayne shoes were classics, and included designs by both André Perugia (see p. 146) and Roger Vivier (see pp. 194–5). All Rayne shoes were made in American sizes. They gained a British Royal Warrant in 1935, made Queen Elizabeth II's wedding shoes in 1947 and pioneered a Wedgwood jasperware heel in 1958. This stylish heel had a design with a vestal within a wreath and a small cameo on the front, in blue, cream and green variations.

RIGHT: Women's gold mesh, high-cut mules set with diamanté stones, made by H & M Rayne, 1953–9.

By the early 1960s Rayne was manufacturing a modified court shoe design, a reaction at the time to the pointed-toed stiletto, which was starting to lose favour. This new style had a blunt, square toe, often called the 'chisel', while the upper was widened and elongated to make it more spacious and comfortable to wear. It sported a reasonably high, but thick, heel. Vivier designed the toe shape in 1961.

The design was an instant success and found favour on both sides of the Atlantic, especially with such influential types as the Duchess of Windsor and Jacqueline Kennedy. The latter was the epitome of the classic court style, dressing as she did in tailored suits and pillbox hats. An eye-catching characteristic of the design was the addition of a decorative feature to the vamp edge. This could be anything from a diamanté to a rhinestone buckle. In the United States, such shoes were dubbed Pilgrim pumps, after the buckled shoes worn by Puritan pilgrims in the seventeenth century. This name proved rather fanciful, given that the early pilgrims predated buckles by forty years and heels by more than seventy!

RIGHT: A woman's leather court shoe, made by H & M Rayne, 1959. The shoe has a stiletto heel made of distinctive Wedgwood jasperware, featuring a classical figure within a wreath.

LEFT: Women's satin, peep-toed court shoes, made by H & M Rayne during the 1950s.

WINKLEPICKERS AND BROTHEL CREEPERS

The post-war period rapidly became one of experimentation. From 1947 onwards a number of American fashion styles began to gain credence, among them the 'Zoot suit', with its wide-legged and high-waisted trousers paired with a long jacket with padded shoulders.

This style, and others like it, signalled a new individualism and self-determination coupled, for the first time, with the growth of a separate youth market. Post-war young adults wanted to express their freedom, youth and presence.

SHARP, POINTED TOES

For men, a fashion for tapered trousers in the 1950s combined with an exaggerated toe style that was influenced by trends among the black and Hispanic youths of Harlem, New York. The style became known as the winklepicker, a name that derived from the sharp pin used for prying winkles from their shells. The winklepicker bears a distinct resemblance to the medieval poulaine (see pp. 28–9), although twentieth-century versions featured heels. Women, too, wore winklepicker toes on stiletto-heeled court shoes.

THICK CRÊPE SOLES

At the opposite end of the spectrum, a thick crêpe sole with suede upper emerged as a style called the brothel creeper or beetle crusher – the former because a wearer could creep out of a brothel without making a sound and therefore duck payment, and the latter because the thick sole was perfect for crushing small insects!

Brothel creepers were popular with the distinctive Teddy boys of the era, who wore drainpipe trousers, long Edwardian-style jackets with velvet collars and skinny ties. *The Shoe and Leather Record* for 13 April 1950 records 'Bold Look. The demand for a more spectacular man's shoe is not confined to the young or…otherwise loudly-dressed custom? Great demand for crepe sole wedge heel…must be full in the toe. Tan upper to take antique dressing'.

Why crêpe? It was relatively cheap and hard-wearing, with a large amount of elasticity, durability and non-slip properties (although such requirements were hardly in demand at the time). Maybe men were attracted to the added height? The style certainly offered a complete contrast to the winklepicker.

OPPOSITE: Exquisite men's grey, pearlized, imitation crocodile and black calf buckle winklepickers, styled in Italy by Ideal Shoemakers, 1960. These British-made shoes imitated Italian style at a fraction of the cost.

BELOW: Men's leather and crêpe rubber-soled brothel creepers, *c.* 1950–5.

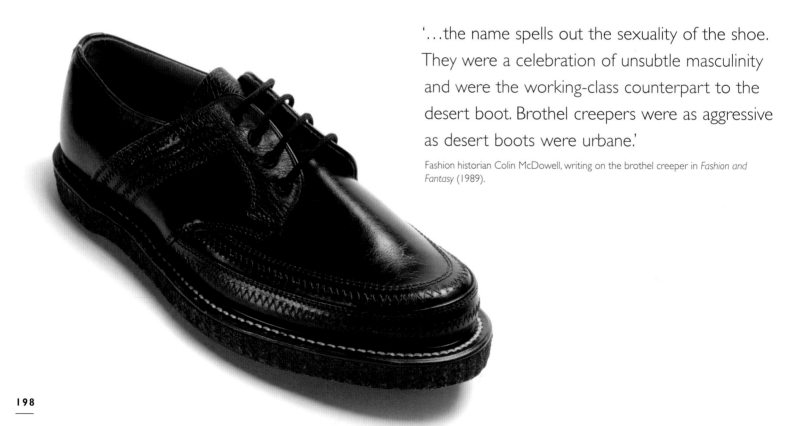

'…the name spells out the sexuality of the shoe. They were a celebration of unsubtle masculinity and were the working-class counterpart to the desert boot. Brothel creepers were as aggressive as desert boots were urbane.'

Fashion historian Colin McDowell, writing on the brothel creeper in *Fashion and Fantasy* (1989).

THE RISE OF THE TEENAGER
AN AIR OF REBELLION

At the beginning of the 1950s, few people realized that the world was entering a more vigorous and changeable time. The first half of the decade had been a conservative one, with people trying to adjust to change following the Second World War. But a reaction to pre-war austerity combined with increased prosperity and advances in technology meant that a revolution was about to happen.

As the decade progressed, increased optimism met with the tidal wave of new music from America – Rock 'n' Roll. This exciting and, to many, dangerous new musical style exploded onto the scene with Bill Haley and His Comets singing 'Rock Around the Clock'. Such music, and the clothes that band members wore, began to influence young people in their aspirations, desires and wardrobe.

TEENAGE TENDENCIES
Growing up pre-war meant being serious – a mini version of Mum and Dad, if you like, but how old-fashioned this had now become. The 'teenager' was born – an individual in his or her own right who could follow a different lifestyle to that of his or her parents' generation. The old stuffy rules and traditions that once governed how one lived one's life – what one wore and how one behaved – relaxed and could be abandoned altogether by following the fashion trends that were strongly linked to this new music.
    American actors, Marlon Brando in *The Wild One* and James Dean in *Rebel Without a Cause*, provided dangerous yet exciting images of what the new look could be. Blue denim jeans, black leather jackets and sneakers. Who could not be seduced by Dean's insouciant charm?

NEW SHOES
Dance floors were filled with ponytailed girls in full, knee-length skirts over layers of net petticoats worn with white bobby socks and flat, ballerina-style, slip-on shoes. Boys wore T-shirts and jeans. Such youthful fashions required youthful shoes. The flat, ballerina style was simple and fresh – and popularized by Audrey Hepburn who wore a pair in the film *Funny Face* (1957). The low-heeled, laced saddle shoe was also popular and came in two-tone colours – usually white with a black saddle. Both styles were a rebel response to a girl's mother's high-heeled stiletto.

ABOVE: American teeangers going steady and dancing at a friend's house, 1954.

LEFT: Men's blue and white flecked canvas 'sneaker' boot, made by British firm Clark & Sons Ltd, 1965–6.

LEFT: Men's corduroy lace desert-style boots with a rubber sole and low heel. Made in Italy, 1964.

KINKY BOOTS

The 1960s heralded a new world full of adventure and exciting possibilities. The miniskirt, the epitome of Swinging Sixties fashion, focused attention on the slim youthful leg, but also on footwear. 'Legs never had it so good,' trumpeted the British press.

KNEE-HIGH BOOTS

This was the era of the 'kinky' boot, epitomized in England by a knee-high, black leather boot that took its inspiration from the underground world of fetish clubs. Roger Vivier (see pp. 194–5) was influenced by historical cussarde boots – thigh-high military boots from the seventeenth century – and made them for many celebrities, including Rudolf Nureyev. Such boots were also worn by the model girlfriends of rock stars and on TV by Honor Blackman as Cathy Gale and Diana Rigg as Emma Peel in *The Avengers*.

Across the Atlantic, the American Go-Go boot took its name from an American discotheque, Whisky a Go Go in Chicago and Hollywood. The style involved a calf-high boot, which then developed in to a knee-high version towards the end of the 1960s. Both incarnations had a blunt, squared-off toe. Different versions existed, with side- or back-zip fastenings and, later, elasticated tops. Sometimes Go-Go boots were front-laced. All versions had a flat or low heel.

Also from the United States came a classic stretch boot designed by Beth and Herbert Levine. It looked much like a stocking with a clear acrylic heel. The couple even designed an all-in-one boot-and-trouser ensemble.

'Full length, half length,

Fully fashion calf length,

Brown boots, black boots,

Patent leather jackboots,

Low boots, High boots,

Lovely lanky thigh boots,

We dig all those boots.'

Honor Blackman and co-star Patrick Macnee with their chart success 'Kinky Boots', released by Decca in 1965.

ANKLE BOOTS

The Beatle boot became a popular choice for men – a high-heeled version of the front-seamed Chelsea boot (see pp. 150–1), this time with a pointed toe and high Cuban heel. Tony Calder explained that 'Brian Epstein found these suede boots in a dance shop called Anello and Davide in Mayfair and they were beautifully made, very soft. Because they were dance shoes, of course, they had no soles to speak of, so he had some made with a proper sole and heel and they became known as the Beatle boot.'

The desert boot, designed by Nathan Clark of Clarks, Street, England, became popular in the 1960s. Inspired by the boots designed for soldiers fighting in Burma during the Second World War, the boots were launched at the Chicago Shoe Fair in 1949. It took another fifteen years for them to make it to Europe, but they arrived in time for the student unrest of 1968 and were worn by the Rolling Stones. They were a simple design, with plantation rubber crêpe soles and just two eyelets for laces. It is a style that has remained largely unchanged since that time.

LEFT: Actor Diana Rigg as Emma Peel in *The Avengers*, 1960s. She wears the iconic leather catsuit and a pair of kinky boots.

MARY QUANT

Mary Quant was one of the most influential designers and figures of the 1960s. She started out in 1956, when she and her husband opened their shop, Bazaar, on London's fashionable King's Road. They sold simple, but modern-looking designs – less formal than haute couture styles, but more interesting than mass-produced high-street wares. Of course, Quant's 'hip and happening' new looks needed shoe styles to match.

The overriding styles of this period were catering for the explosion of youth that had started in the 1950s (see pp. 200–1). According to film actress Brigitte Bardot, couture was for 'grandmothers'. Model Twiggy's little girl look was complemented with child-like, low-heeled or flat-bar shoes, often with square toes. White lace tights added to the 'children's party' look. The shoes were a style known as Mary Janes in the United States.

THE SYNTHETICS REVOLUTION

The choice of materials expanded in the 1960s to include fantastic plastics and other synthetics such as Corfam – Dupont's product name for their leather substitute. It first appeared at the Chicago Shoe Show, 1963. Corfam was hard-wearing, kept its shine and was water-repellent. The drawback, however, was that it wasn't as flexible as leather. New synthetic materials were often coated with wet-look finishes or a high, patent-like gloss. Patent leather was very popular in a range of jewel-like colours, including red, green, blue, white and, in particular, aubergine.

Mary Quant introduced her iconic Quant-a-Foot – injection-moulded plastic ankle boots – during this time. Made from clear plastic, they were lined with cotton jersey in bright primary colours. The boots were fun, funky and perfectly matched the miniskirt look. They also sported Quant's trademark daisy impressed into the heel. Along with designer André Courrèges (see pp. 206–7), Quant also went some way towards making the knee-high boot one of the most popular styles of the decade (see pp. 202–3).

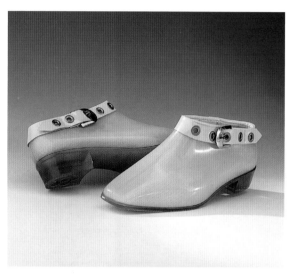

LEFT: Mary Quant's iconic Quant-a-Foot boots in yellow-moulded plastic with a jersey lining, 1967.

LEFT: British model Twiggy wearing a minidress and red patent bar shoes, 1966.

BELOW: Women's purple and black patent bar shoes, 1965. They were made in France, expressly for the British shoe shop, Clifford Turner.

THE SPACE AGE

The 1960s witnessed a race for space between the Soviet Union and the United States, culminating in 1969 with man's first steps on the moon. Fashion designers were massively inspired by the event, in particular French designer André Courrèges, who introduced his 'Space Age' collection in 1964. The collection featured geometric shapes, long shiny white boots, goggles and short skirts made in fluorescent colours from futuristic-looking fabrics.

Courrèges's boots were modern and comfortable and became the iconic boot of the 1960s. They were a shiny white or soft, kid leather slip-on boot with a flat sole or very low heel. Later they were zipped or fastened with Velcro on the inside leg and had squared-off toes. These boots became one of the most widely copied styles of the century, much to the annoyance of Courrèges. Companies including Delman, Ravel and Kurt Geiger turned out similar boots for less money. Lotus, in Northampton, England, produced its own version in black PVC with white stripes – marketed and sold under the Career Brand name.

Pierre Cardin followed suit, introducing a moon-inspired collection in 1967, which took advantage of the new materials available and incorporated plastics, Velcro and high-tech fibres in futuristic whites and silvers.

Paco Rabanne also made space-age clothing in 1966, designing costumes for movies like *Barbarella*, which encouraged the look.

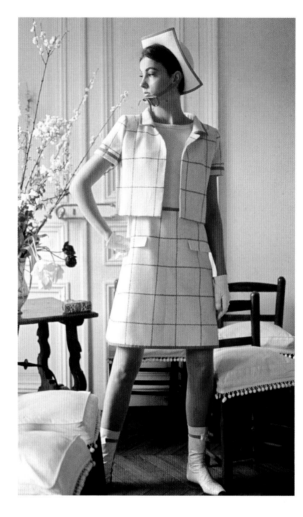

LEFT: A model wears a Courrèges white and orange check skirt suit and hat. A pair of the designer's signature, white, space-age boots completes the look.

OPPOSITE: These iconic, white leather, space-age boots are by Courrèges and date from 1967. They have a softer feel to them than the hard edginess of some of his earlier space-age inspired boots.

FLOWER POWER

Towards the end of the 1960s, the hippy look that had originated on the West Coast of the United States crossed the Atlantic. Mixed feelings about US involvement in the Vietnam War and the rise in consumerism had left many in the United States sceptical and weary. The enthusiasm and vitality of the 1960s began to wane and people started turning to other avenues.

Drug taking increased during this period and the cults and religions from the East became more appealing. In response, designers combined colours, patterns and textures borrowed from non-Western cultures with a bohemian aesthetic. As ethnic influences took over, shoe styles reflected this. A relaxed mix-and-match approach gave rise to long hair for men, cheesecloth bell-bottomed trousers, paisley shirts, face and body paint and lots of beads. Any garment that was loose fitting and could boast of overland journeys from India and Morocco was in.

HIPPY FOOTWEAR

The footwear of choice in this era centred on strappy leather sandals, multicoloured leather or suede patchwork boots – often fringed – and soft leather slip-on shoes. Oriental influences manifested in simple, leather, strappy, almost flat sandals decorated with jewels. Sixties versions of the wooden-soled platform sandals of the Middle East featured regularly in fashion shoots.

Boots became 'psychedelic, man', painted with swirly, otherworldly designs. Styles no longer embraced the stark and streamlined futuristic look of the Space Age (see pp. 206–7), but harked back to earlier, softer, more romantic styles. In the 1970s, boots became known as 'granny boots' for their traditional look.

ABOVE: A term coined by American beat poet Allen Ginsberg, 'flower power' summed up the political sentiment of the age. It later came to represent the hippie movement in general, which embraced free-flowing floral fabrics in bright, sometimes psychedelic, colours.

OPPOSITE: Women's suede, front-lacing boots embroidered with a floral design in coloured cotton thread, c. 1974. The embroidery was carried out by the Greek workshops of Jerry Edouard Jerrold for Kurt Geiger.

BOOGIE NIGHTS

'Monster boots with vast club like wedges, weighty legacies from the hideous Victoriana of Lancashire Mills' was the verdict of London-based newspaper *The Times* in 1971. Funky and glamorous or ridiculous and impractical? The platform shoe epitomized the 1970s, the decade that many people think fashion forgot. To others this is the last truly recognizable new style that was around for more than a bat of an eye.

Shoe designers reintroduced the platform from as early as 1967. The last time it had been seen was on footwear of the 1930s and 1940s (see pp. 170–1). Before that, it had been a feature of the medieval Venetian chopine (see pp. 30–1). Platforms for both men and women rose to ridiculous heights, particularly those worn by such glam-rock legends as Elton John and David Bowie, who tottered around on 15–18 cm (7–8 in) silver stacks. In London, Biba owner Barbara Hulanicki and the designer Terry de Havilland (see pp. 212–13) popularized platform shoes.

PLATFORMS AND FLARES

Not everyone was into 'glam' fashions, yet the impractical and over-the-top platform filtered down to the high street, where both men and women chose to wear them. Coupled with the flared trouser, it created a singular look. A moderate platform sole had elegance, but as the platforms grew in size, they became distorted and disproportionate to the legs, making the wearer look as if he or she was wearing orthopaedic shoes. A British Pathé News clip of the time reports: 'Well they don't look very safe to me and I don't know what they do to your feet but the manufacturers and the fashion editors say, "Not to worry, they look great"'.

A wide variety of materials were used in producing the striking looks of this era – metallic leathers, cork, crêpe rubber, textured textiles, rope-, leather- or plastic-covered wood. Wooden platform-soled clog mules, or slides as they were known in the United States, were very popular, though some reached amazingly chunky heights.

LEFT: Fashion models, including Marie Helvin (right) wear funky, short jumpsuits and high-boot platforms created by the Japanese designer Kansai Yamamoto.

OPPOSITE: A pair of women's silver leather buckle shoes with a platform sole and amazing flared heel. This pair was designed by Canadian John Fluevog for Sacha, c. 1975, and epitomizes the eccentricity of the disco age.

A popular brand of cork-soled sandal was the Kork-Ease from the United States, seen in the mall and on certain celebrities of the day who appreciated their casual yet striking natural leather straps combined with a lightweight cork platform.

A cartoon from the 1970s depicts a woman in a pair of high platform shoes about to be arrested. She shouts to the policeman 'Come any closer and I'll jump!' By early 1974, the craze for platforms had started to diminish. Eventually, women were once again wearing feminine high heels and there was not a platform in sight.

'I just can't imagine fancying a chick in flat shoes…'

Terry de Havilland.

TERRY DE HAVILLAND

One of the iconic designers and shoemakers of the 1970s and still 'cobbling' today, Terry de Havilland has created some of the most feminine yet sexily outrageous shoes of the last forty years. Rock chicks past and present still clamour at his door.

De Havilland's metallic leather and exotic-skinned platform-soled sandals sum up the glamour of the 1970s and highlight a brief flirtation with the use of exotic skins – including snakeskin – that several designers embraced at this time.

De Havilland had worked in his father's shoe factory, Waverley Shoes, in the West End of London. Following a brief sojourn to Italy, de Havilland had, by the 1960s, taken control of his father's factory, where he began to design and make his own unique styles. All the shoes he made had high heels or wedges – some higher than others. His trademark designs used snakeskin, either dyed or in a metallic finish. A number of his most enduring styles date from 1969 and include a three-tiered wedge with an ankle strap called the Leyla. By 1972 de Havilland had opened a shop on the King's Road, London, calling it 'Cobblers to the World'.

CONSTANTLY EVOLVING

De Havilland's shoes were incredibly sought after and worn by all the cool dudes of the age, including Bianca Jagger, Anita Pallenburg, Angie and David Bowie and today, Kate Moss. He designed Tim Curry's shoes for the *Rocky Horror Picture Show*, brought back the stiletto for a Zandra Rhodes catwalk show, and made red, silk-lined black leather thigh boots for Jackie Onassis. His almost dream-like designs included the famous Zebedee, which hit the market in 1979. It was a mule with two suede straps across the toes and a lightning flash. The heel made an amazing corkscrew effect, fashioned in metal wire. The shoe came in different colourways including black suede with a gold flash.

In the late 1970s, de Havilland found himself competing with the punk aesthetic and his glamorous shoes fell out of favour. He went underground and formed Kamikaze shoes, making footwear for the goth and fetish scene. Styles included heavily buckled winklepickers adorned with skulls, studs and spikes. De Havilland then established the Magic Shoe Company, making the most amazing holographic platform boots. This was successful, but financial and health problems forced him to take a back seat. Like all good things, the designer is back today and continues to make platforms and wedges in his inimitable style.

ABOVE: British model, Kate Moss, poses in a pair of high wedge-heeled de Havilland's for the opening of his London store, April 2013.

BELOW: The perfect shoe for a disco diva, these striking green metallic-leather and mock-crocodile, ankle-strap platform sandals were designed and made by Terry de Havilland, c. 1975.

THE PUNK EXPLOSION
GOD SAVE THE QUEEN

Punk exploded onto the scene in 1976 and dominated the following year, with the Sex Pistols' anthem 'God Save the Queen' providing the anarchic soundtrack for Queen Elizabeth's Silver Jubilee.

Wearing clothing that was deliberately shocking – ripped and safety-pinned T-shirts bearing irreverent slogans, bondage trousers with bum flaps – and having hair fashioned into colourful spikes or a Mohican became an expression of the punk movement's disgust at middle-class aspiration and the bland music scene of teeny-boppers and glam rockers.

The punk's choice of footwear was equally mixed, and ranged from crêpe-soled creepers and pointed winkle-pickers to stilettos and Dr Martens. Punks often created their look by throwing together wildly unrelated items. It was creation out of disorder. A look pulled together on the street is hard to pin down style-wise, but street-style critic Ted Polhemus unearthed adverts for Bloggs of London who were advertising 'The Rebel Boot…made especially for anti-establishment heroines!' and Trouble Makers with a 'cult ankle chain and safety pin buckle – boots to dictate by.' All had the subversive stiletto heel.

BONDAGE GEAR

Designers Vivienne Westwood (see pp. 234–5) and partner Malcolm McLaren had a shop on London's King's Road, which, by 1974, they had named 'Sex'. They introduced a bondage collection in which they covered black leather and fabric clothing with straps, zips, studs, buckles and chains Westwood's shoe collection at the time contained bondage boots covered in straps and buckles that complemented the bondage trousers and the look in general.

RIGHT: The punk uniform: bleached, spiked hair; Union Jack T-shirt, ripped tights, studded dog collars and, of course, a pair of multi-hole Dr Martens boots.

LEFT: Men's black suede and mock-leopard-skin monk shoe, branded 'Cowboy' design, and made by Vincent Shoes Ltd, Leicester, England, 1975–80s. Animal prints, such as leopard skin, featured widely in fashion during the 1980s.

DR MARTENS

Are Doc Martens boots for all people? What started out as a boot to promote health has, over the years, been everything from a working man's boot to a fashion icon. Adopted by such diverse groups as punks, mods and skinheads, the Dr Martens story is something of a rollercoaster ride.

Anyone who has owned a pair of Dr Martens in the past feels a stab of nostalgia when he or she sees them on the feet of others – that is, of course, unless he or she still wears them!

HUMBLE ORIGINS

Dr Martens have a strong sense of heritage and yet at the same time are as contemporary as any of today's latest styles. The origins of this shoe go back to a certain Dr Klaus Märtens who, while on holiday in 1945, injured his ankle skiing. He couldn't find a suitable boot to wear and so designed his own made from soft leather with an air-cushioned sole. Hardly establishing a commercial venture, he went into partnership with his old friend Dr Herbert Funck and they started to manufacture the footwear, selling them as comfortable shoes that were good for the feet.

DM SUCCESS

By 1959 the company had grown so large that Märtens and Funck were looking to expand internationally. British shoe manufacturer the R Griggs Group Ltd, Wollaston, Northamptonshire, bought the patent rights to manufacture the shoes in the United Kingdom. Changing the name, reshaping the heel, adding what has become the trademark yellow stitching and AirWair soles, the first Dr Martens boots rolled off the production line on 1 April 1960, hence the name of the 1460 style, the iconic, eight-eyelet, front-lacing ankle boot in ox blood. (The 1 represents the 1st and the 4 represents the month of April, so 1460 signifies 1 April 1960, the date of the first Dr Martens boot.)

AN ALL-PURPOSE BOOT

These boots were perfect practical wear for professions such as postmen, the police and factory workers. Since their launch in the United Kingdom, all people have worn the boots, from students and punks to mums and dads. Not everyone likes them – for some it is too masculine and rather plain – but the boot nevertheless became one of the defining styles of footwear in the latter half of the twentieth century.

BELOW: The classic and iconic 1460 eight eyelet cherry red Dr Marten boot. So named as the original first boot rolled off the production line on 1 April 1960.

RIGHT: Always forward looking and innovative, R Griggs Group, the manufacturers of Dr Marten footwear, have come up with these stunning women's brogues, made from Anilmorbido leather which has a high shiny metallic finish. It's been combined with Byzantium silk to create an intriguing combination. The silk is a high quality bespoke silk pattern woven in Stephen Walters & Son's mill, Suffolk, UK, 2011.

THE NEW MUST-HAVE ACCESSORY

Trainers, joggers, runners, gutties, sneakers, pumps, plimsolls, skiffs, high tops, fishheads, bobos, bumpers, cleats, sannies or dappers – what do you call yours?

Up until the 1970s, even with the rise of such legendary brands as Dunlop's 'Green Flash', Converse and Keds (see pp. 128–9, 148–9), sneakers were still predominately worn by sportsmen and women for comfort and to enhance athletic performance. By the 1970s, however, the wearing of sports shoes was starting to change as emerging marketing-driven companies such as adidas, Puma and Nike took on the more traditional producers of sports shoes. The former, while producing specialized shoes for individual sports, had started to realize that increasing financial gain and worldwide domination was available to them simply by turning the humble sports shoe into an essential, wearable item for contemporary living.

CELEBRITY ENDORSEMENT

Pressure rose when companies began to use individual sportsmen and women in their advertising campaigns. Fans became more interested in what their heroes and heroines were wearing on their feet and how they wore them. By the late 1970s Puma's advertising campaigns had a two-pronged approach, focusing on 'basketball players' and 'casual wearers', with the increasing recognition that the latter were streaking ahead in terms of purchasing power.

What was once a generic sports shoe was, all of a sudden, simultaneously targeted not only at a wide range of different sports, but also at the new youth market and the burgeoning leisure market. There were sneakers for basketball, aerobics, cross training, skateboarding, tennis, dance party culture and the hip-hop scene.

FITNESS FREAKS

The aerobics and jogging crazes of the 1970s and 1980s created a Western obsession with exercise. Health and fitness became synonymous with enhanced attractiveness and success. The sneaker was a key enhancing item. Reebok took the market lead from Nike when they backed the aerobics craze and produced a sneaker specifically aimed at women. Nike's 1977 slogan, 'there is no finish line',

committed Nike wearers to a lifetime pursuit of self-improvement – not to mention a lifetime of keeping up with the latest styles!

The idea that the consumer could choose a brand of sneaker solely based on its image and sporting celebrity associations gained momentum. Greater variety was not enough – buyers made lifestyle choices, too. Sneakers were now promoted as a panacea to everyday problems and became a must-have of daily life. They could improve your performance, make you fit, make you look good, make you successful, make you more attractive to girls or boys and they could make you every bit as cool as your sporting and celebrity heroes.

ABOVE: Aerobics became the buzz word of mid-1980s fitness. Women (mostly) throughout the Western world stepped, jumped and squatted to the beats of the latest sounds in pop music.

RIGHT: Women's suede and textile Nike Aloha sneakers, 1979–80. From a technical point of view, this is a rather basic model, but the outstanding floral pattern and limited release made this one of the most sought-after models of the time.

THE SHOE AS ART
YOU CAN LOOK, BUT DON'T TOUCH

Shoes are practical, they can be truly beautiful and, as in the 1970s, they can be works of art. It was during this decade that shoes became embraced as sculptural art forms – a little tongue in cheek, perhaps, but always playful and fun. A number of art styles could still be worn, although many of them were purely decorative.

The 1979 Crafts Council Shoe Show: British Shoes Since 1790 highlighted an obsession with shoes that surprised many. People showed interest, not only in shoe style and history, but also in the fact that shoes could be turned into something magical and sculptural.

THEA CADABRA

Thea Cadabra's fantasy shoes from the 1970s are sold as wearable art. Her maxim was, 'Wearing wonderful shoes is a truly uplifting experience'. Cadabra's designs carried themes and featured three-dimensional motifs that lent drama to her creations. Best known among her designs are the Cloud and Rainbow, the Dragon, the Maid and the Bat. The Cloud and Rainbow is an amazing shoe, essentially a court shoe in blue suede, which has been skilfully accessorized with a leather rainbow and little beads symbolizing the rain.

GAZA BOWEN

Internationally renowned sculptor Gaza Bowen has exhibited extensively since 1978. In the broadest sense her work is an enquiry into the non-verbal communication between people and objects, and for nearly twenty years she has focused her attention on shoes: their construction, history, cultural meaning and social significance. She made the Red Shoe Reader and her famous Tuff Scuffs – feminine mules adorned with scouring pads!

CANDACE BAHOUTH

Candace Bahouth designed and created the amazing Winter and Spring boots with technical help from Walker's Shoes; they were commissioned by the Crafts Council in 1979. These boots are made from pink tapestry decorated with appropriate winter and spring accessories – so spring flowers and birds or winter birds and flowers in frosty looking colours. Complete with synthetic, green grass wedge heels, they were not practical for wearing.

OPPOSITE: Gaza Bowen's Red Shoe Reader, 1994. The shoe is constructed from a red leather, stiletto-heeled court shoe, cut at the back of the forepart and with a concertina-page book inserted between the two halves. The book pages feature images and text relating to high-heeled shoes.

ABOVE: Thea Cadabra's Cloud and Rainbow, 1979. Pink and yellow clouds issue raindrops made from strings of beads and a lightning flash in silver leather is attached to the centre of the vamp.